MAYER SMITH

My Lonely Holiday

Copyright © 2024 by Mayer Smith

All rights reserved. No part of this publication may be reproduced, stored or transmitted in any form or by any means, electronic, mechanical, photocopying, recording, scanning, or otherwise without written permission from the publisher. It is illegal to copy this book, post it to a website, or distribute it by any other means without permission.

This novel is entirely a work of fiction. The names, characters and incidents portrayed in it are the work of the author's imagination. Any resemblance to actual persons, living or dead, events or localities is entirely coincidental.

Mayer Smith asserts the moral right to be identified as the author of this work.

Mayer Smith has no responsibility for the persistence or accuracy of URLs for external or third-party Internet Websites referred to in this publication and does not guarantee that any content on such Websites is, or will remain, accurate or appropriate.

Designations used by companies to distinguish their products are often claimed as trademarks. All brand names and product names used in this book and on its cover are trade names, service marks, trademarks and registered trademarks of their respective owners. The publishers and the book are not associated with any product or vendor mentioned in this book. None of the companies referenced within the book have endorsed the book.

First edition

This book was professionally typeset on Reedsy. Find out more at reedsy.com

Contents

1	The Unexpected Invitation	1
2	A Cold Welcome	8
3	The Weight of Silence	15
4	Beneath the Surface	22
5	Through the Mist	29
6	The Eyes Beneath the Stone	36
7	The Depths of Desire	42
8	The Shattered Path	49
9	The Echoes of Betrayal	57
10	The Whispering Depths	64
11	Beneath the Surface	71
12	The Weight of the Dark	78
13	The Waking Nightmare	85
14	The Breaking Point	92
15	The Fractured Reflection	99
16	The Edge of All Things	106
17	The Hollow Within	113
18	Fragments of the Fallen	120
19	The Flicker of Hope	128
20	Into the Light	135
21	Echoes of the Past	143
22	The Veil of Shadows	150
23	The Edge of Madness	156
24	The Breaking Point	163

25	The Gatekeeper's Promise	170
26	The Choice of Darkness	177
27	The Breaking Point	184
28	Into the Abyss	191
29	The Final Hour	197
30	The Heart of the Hollow	203
31	Into the Light	210

1

The Unexpected Invitation

Eleanor Westwood had always preferred the quiet hum of the city to the whisper of nature. The bustling streets, the anonymity of a thousand faces, the rhythmic pulse of urban life—it was where she felt most alive, or perhaps, most comfortable. But on that particularly rainy Tuesday morning, everything had changed. The letter had come.

The letter was thick, ivory in color, and sealed with a dark crimson wax. Eleanor had been sitting at her kitchen table, the steam from her coffee curling like tendrils into the air, when she first noticed it. At first glance, it appeared entirely out of place. The only mail she received these days was either from work—immediately forgotten once the envelope was torn open—or from her mother, who still insisted on sending handwritten notes to her adult daughter in a world of instant messaging.

But this letter... this one was different.

It lay on the counter, almost waiting for her. As if it knew she would find it.

With no return address, no indication of who might have sent it, she felt a shiver dance down her spine. Her fingers hovered over the envelope for a moment longer than necessary, as if the act of opening it would somehow reveal more than just ink on paper. But curiosity had always been her greatest weakness.

She sliced the envelope open with a small knife she used for letters—sharp, precise. The paper inside was smooth to the touch, heavier than the usual correspondence. Unfolding it, she saw words written in a delicate, flowing hand.

Dear Miss Westwood,

You are cordially invited to a secluded retreat in the heart of the Blue Ridge Mountains. Here, amidst the untouched beauty of the forest, you will find the space to reconnect with yourself, to silence the noise of the world, and to find peace in the solitude. The cabin awaits your arrival.

Please find enclosed the details of your travel arrangements. You will be expected in three days.

With warm regards,

A Friend

There was no name. No explanation. Just the promise of some kind of retreat—a place of solitude. The words on the page, though elegant and soothing, did little to calm the increasing unease creeping over Eleanor.

She had never heard of any place like this retreat. The Blue Ridge Mountains were over six hours away, far beyond the places she usually visited. And as for the name of the sender... it was all too vague. But something about the letter called to her. It was as though it knew what she needed before she did.

Eleanor glanced at the small, folded slip of paper that had accompanied the letter. The train ticket was already arranged for her, departing in three days. The details of the journey seemed legitimate, even though she didn't recognize the name of the cabin's location. A tiny wrinkle of doubt pressed between her brows, but it was quickly pushed aside by the allure of something different, something new.

It wasn't the first time she'd found herself looking for an escape. The last year had been difficult, to say the least. Work was wearing her thin, her social life non-existent, and her mother's occasional guilt trips about "settling down" were beginning to wear her out. She needed a break—needed to breathe, away from the noise, the constant buzz of responsibilities and expectations.

Eleanor took a slow breath, weighing the pros and cons. There was something enticing about the idea, something almost... liberating. She needed to escape. She needed this. Or perhaps she was simply convincing herself.

Perhaps I should go, she thought, the decision beginning to take shape in her mind. It's only three days. It could be exactly what I need.

Three days later, Eleanor found herself standing on the platform of a small, almost forgotten train station, her suitcase by her side and the ticket clutched tightly in her hand. The morning air was sharp, tingling against her skin, and there was a weight in her chest that didn't quite make sense. The train was late. That didn't surprise her—everything was late these days.

When the train finally arrived, it looked older than she expected. The metal sides were scuffed, the paint chipped and faded, and the windows fogged over with the dampness of the morning. But it wasn't the train itself that unsettled her. It was the lack of people. There was no bustle, no thrumming of the usual commuters. Just a few scattered figures, dressed in dark coats, standing with their heads turned downward, avoiding eye contact.

Eleanor swallowed, her palms suddenly slick with sweat, but she boarded the train without a second thought. There was no going back now. The cabin, whatever it was, awaited her.

The ride was long and quiet. Occasionally, the train would jerk as if protesting its age, but for the most part, the journey was uneventful. Outside, the world grew darker and quieter with every passing mile. The landscape slowly shifted from the familiar concrete of the city to open, undisturbed fields, and eventually to dense, almost impenetrable woods.

Around midnight, the train finally slowed to a halt at a station that didn't seem to belong anywhere. There was no sign, no light except the faint glow of an old lamp hanging by the platform.

A man stood there, waiting.

He was tall, dressed in a heavy coat that seemed to absorb the shadows. His face was sharp, angular, with features that felt almost... too perfect. His eyes, dark and unreadable, caught Eleanor's gaze as she disembarked from the train.

"You must be Miss Westwood," he said, his voice low and steady.

"Yes, I am," Eleanor replied, her throat tightening as she stepped down onto the platform.

The man didn't smile. He merely nodded, taking her suitcase from her with a smooth, almost practiced motion. His silence made Eleanor uncomfortable, but she followed him, unable to ignore the sense that the world was slowly shifting around her.

The journey to the cabin was brief, but the further they walked into the woods, the more unsettling it became. The trees, tall and twisted, seemed to close in on them, casting long shadows that stretched and crept like fingers reaching for her. The man walked ahead without looking back, his strides sure, confident. Eleanor, however, couldn't shake the feeling that they were being watched.

Finally, after what felt like an eternity, the man stopped in front of a small, dark building. The cabin was quaint, but something about it felt wrong—wrong in a way she couldn't quite place. The wood was old, weather-beaten, and covered in a thick layer of ivy. The door, slightly ajar, creaked as the man pushed it open.

"This is your home for the next few days," he said simply, his voice distant.

Eleanor didn't reply immediately. She stepped over the threshold and into the dim light of the cabin. The air inside was thick, heavy with the smell of pine and something more... ancient, as if the very walls held secrets they were reluctant to share.

The man set her suitcase down beside the fireplace, which had long since gone cold. Without a word, he turned and left, disappearing into the darkness outside.

Eleanor stood alone in the cabin, the door creaking shut behind her. The stillness pressed in, suffocating her. She tried to shake it off, reminding herself that she had chosen this. The invitation had been clear. The retreat was meant to help her heal, to help her find peace. But the eerie silence, the cold touch of the cabin, made it feel like something else entirely.

For the first time, Eleanor wondered if she had made a mistake.

But it was too late now. She was alone in the mountains, and she couldn't turn back. Not yet.

The letter had promised solitude. What it hadn't warned her

about was how quickly solitude could begin to feel like something else—something darker, something more dangerous.

The fire crackled faintly in the hearth.

And outside, the wind whispered her name.

2

A Cold Welcome

Eleanor woke in the dead of night, the sound of the wind howling through the trees like an ancient, mournful cry. Her eyes snapped open, heart racing. The dream she had just woken from—a blurry, fractured memory—lingered at the edges of her mind. It was too hazy to recall, but the sensation it left behind was unmistakable. It was fear. A deep, primal fear.

She sat up in the bed, her body trembling slightly from the cold, though the fire she had started earlier in the hearth still burned low. It was enough to cast long shadows across the small, rustic cabin, the flames flickering like ghosts across the wooden walls. She had tucked herself into bed hours ago, the overwhelming silence of the cabin making her retreat into the warmth of the blankets. But now... now it felt like the house was watching her.

The wind outside had picked up again, and the long, drawn-out moan of the trees made the cabin seem less like a sanctuary and more like a tomb. She hugged the blanket tighter around her shoulders, feeling the chill seep into her bones despite the warmth of the fire.

She glanced over at the dimly lit doorway. The light from the fire barely reached the edge of the room, and the darkness beyond it was thick—impenetrable.

She had heard the wind earlier, too. It sounded different in the mountains. The howling, the low rumble like the earth itself was trying to speak, was constant. Yet something else felt off. Like an unsettling rhythm, a pulse. Her mind was playing tricks on her, no doubt.

Shaking her head, she pulled herself out of bed and padded quietly over to the window. It was only then that she realized how deeply the night had fallen. The moon, pale and full, bathed the forest in a cold, silver light. The trees, tall and menacing, swayed violently against the wind, their branches reaching toward the cabin like fingers from a nightmare. Her breath fogged up the glass as she leaned closer, straining her eyes to see past the shadows.

For a moment, there was nothing. Just the swirling mist from the mountain, rolling thick and low, blurring the line between sky and earth. But then, something caught her eye.

A figure.

At the edge of the forest, near the line of trees, a man stood. His silhouette was unmistakable—tall, thin, and draped in a heavy coat. His face was hidden in the shadows, but Eleanor knew it was the man who had greeted her when she arrived. The one who had brought her here.

Her heart skipped a beat. He was standing still, as though waiting for something. His posture was rigid, almost unnaturally so, and though she couldn't see his expression, something in the way he stood made her feel like he was watching her.

The hairs on the back of her neck stood on end.

She stumbled back from the window, her pulse quickening. What was he doing out there?

But as quickly as she had seen him, the figure was gone. Disappeared into the night, swallowed by the trees and the darkness beyond. Eleanor pressed her palms to the cool glass, trying to calm the erratic beating of her heart. She wasn't sure what she had just seen—or if she had even seen it at all—but the sensation of being watched lingered. It clung to her like the fog rolling in from the forest, thick and suffocating.

Her eyes flicked to the door.

The cabin was eerily still. The fire crackled softly in the hearth, its glow casting dancing shadows on the walls. She hesitated, her breath shallow. There was no reason to be afraid. She was alone. She was supposed to be alone. The retreat was meant to be peaceful, to allow her to find clarity away from the chaos of the city. Yet, her instincts screamed that something wasn't right.

Unable to shake the feeling of unease, Eleanor pulled on her thick sweater and slipped her feet into a pair of boots. She had no real plan, but she needed to do something, to move.

The wind howled louder as she opened the door and stepped out into the cold, her breath turning to mist in the night air. The wind carried with it the scent of pine and damp earth, sharp and unsettling. The forest, thick and oppressive, loomed in every direction. A low fog rolled in from the trees, blanketing the ground in a sea of white.

Eleanor hesitated, looking back at the warmth of the cabin, but something—some instinct—pulled her forward. She couldn't explain why. It wasn't as though she believed the man outside was anything other than a figment of her imagination. He had vanished, after all.

And yet, there was something in the air tonight. The fog, the wind, the sense of something moving just beyond the trees. Something watching her.

She took a few hesitant steps forward, her boots crunching against the frost-bitten ground, and then stopped. At the edge of the forest, just out of the corner of her eye, she saw something—something moving between the trees. She whirled, but the figure was gone. The fog, thick as it was, swallowed whatever had been there.

Her heart hammered in her chest as she stood frozen, her breath shallow. She was imagining things. Of course, she was. It was the isolation, the quiet that made her mind play tricks on her.

Still, she couldn't shake the feeling of being watched.

She turned back toward the cabin and, in the distance, saw the man again.

This time, though, he wasn't alone.

Two others stood beside him—figures cloaked in shadows, their features indistinct. They were standing by the trees, looking toward her cabin. She was certain they could see her. A shiver ran down her spine. The figures moved closer to the edge of the forest, and Eleanor stepped back, her instincts screaming at her to run, to lock the door, to stay inside where it was safe.

But as she turned to hurry back, the ground beneath her feet shifted. She slipped, falling hard onto the icy soil. Pain shot through her side, and for a moment, she lay there, winded and breathless, staring up at the sky above. The stars had disappeared behind a heavy veil of clouds, and the moonlight was dimmed by the creeping fog.

When she looked back toward the trees, the figures were gone. No trace. No sign they had ever been there.

Confused, disoriented, she scrambled to her feet, brushing off the dirt and leaves that clung to her clothes. Her breath was ragged, and her heart raced with the remnants of fear. What had just happened? Had she imagined it? Or was something else at play here, something she couldn't yet understand?

A sharp sound—a creak from the cabin door—caught her

attention. Her blood ran cold.

Someone had opened the door.

Slowly, Eleanor turned, her pulse thudding in her ears. She moved toward the door, instinctively pulling the collar of her sweater tighter around her neck. Her breath came out in uneven bursts, her mind spinning with the possibilities of what could be waiting for her inside.

The door creaked wider.

And then, standing in the dim light of the cabin, was the man.

He was not alone.

Behind him stood another figure—one that she hadn't seen before. A woman, tall and thin, with sharp, penetrating eyes. She wore a coat as dark as midnight, her hair tangled and wild as if she had just come from the woods. She stared at Eleanor with an intensity that made her blood freeze in her veins.

Without a word, the man stepped aside, letting the woman move toward Eleanor.

For a long, heart-stopping moment, Eleanor stood in the threshold, the weight of their gaze pressing down on her. And then, the woman spoke, her voice cold and smooth like ice.

"You shouldn't have come," she said.

And Eleanor, standing frozen in place, realized with a sickening certainty that she was no longer alone in the mountains. She wasn't just here for a retreat.

She was part of something far darker than she had ever imagined.

3

The Weight of Silence

Eleanor's heart thudded painfully against her ribs as the woman's words settled into the air, thick with foreboding. The door to the cabin loomed behind her like an open mouth, dark and silent. She glanced at the man who had greeted her upon arrival, standing in the doorway, his face unreadable. His silence, as cold and impenetrable as the mountain air, seemed to suffocate her.

"You shouldn't have come," the woman repeated, her voice steady but carrying a weight that made Eleanor's skin crawl. There was no malice in her tone, no visible anger, but something about the way she spoke made Eleanor feel as though she had unknowingly crossed some invisible line.

The wind howled from the trees, the mist now creeping in closer, wrapping around the edges of the cabin like the tendrils of some unseen predator. Eleanor's breath came in shallow, ragged gasps, her body frozen in place as she tried to make sense of the situation. She had expected isolation, quiet, maybe even a sense of peace. What she hadn't anticipated was this—this strange, unsettling presence that now pressed in from all sides.

"I'm sorry," Eleanor said, her voice shaky, though she fought to keep her composure. "I don't understand. Who are you?"

The woman's eyes flashed, and for a moment, Eleanor saw something—an unreadable flicker—before the woman's lips curved into a thin, almost imperceptible smile.

"Does it matter who we are?" the woman replied, stepping closer. "You've already made your choice. And now you must live with it."

Eleanor took a step back, her feet shifting on the frost-covered ground. She had to get control, had to make sense of this. The retreat, the invitation—it was supposed to be a haven, not this. Not... this.

"Look, I just arrived here to get away from everything," Eleanor said, her voice wavering as she tried to force some clarity into the conversation. "I don't want any trouble. I just... I just need some time alone."

The woman didn't respond right away. Instead, she took another step forward, her movements deliberate and calculated. Eleanor's breath caught in her throat. There was no hostility in her posture, but there was something far more unnerving: an undeniable sense of authority. The woman was in control here, and she knew it.

"Time alone?" The woman's eyes narrowed slightly. "You've come to the wrong place for that."

A cold shiver ran down Eleanor's spine. What did that mean?

Before she could respond, the man in the doorway spoke, his voice low and steady, cutting through the tension like a knife.

"Come inside, Miss Westwood," he said, his gaze fixed on her, unwavering. "It's too late to go back now."

The finality in his voice made her blood run cold. Eleanor had been debating whether she should flee, whether she should just leave, but now, faced with the man's command and the woman's silent menace, her legs felt rooted to the spot. She wanted to scream, to demand answers, but all she could do was stand there, numb and paralyzed by the sudden weight of fear.

She forced herself to take a hesitant step forward, then another. She had no idea why she was moving toward the cabin—was it fear that kept her walking, or something else? Some strange magnetism drawing her in? Either way, she was too far gone.

The man stepped aside, allowing her to pass through the doorway. As she crossed the threshold, the chill of the outside world seemed to linger, curling around her as if the very walls of the cabin were trying to keep her trapped within.

The woman entered right behind her, closing the door softly behind her. The sound of it locking echoed in the small, dimly lit room, making Eleanor's stomach tighten with dread.

The cabin was smaller than she had expected. There was a large stone fireplace along the far wall, with an almost nonchalant fire burning low, casting flickering shadows on the wooden beams above. The air inside smelled of pine, aged wood, and something else, something faintly metallic that she couldn't quite place. The walls were bare, save for a few old, faded photographs that hung askew. The furniture was simple, unremarkable, except for the heavy, dark chairs that seemed to dominate the room.

It was as if the cabin was waiting for something. Waiting for her.

Eleanor stood in the middle of the room, unsure of what to do next. She wanted to ask more questions, to demand answers, but the weight of the woman's gaze made her feel like she was walking on fragile ground.

She turned back to the man and the woman, both of them now standing by the hearth. Their silence spoke louder than words ever could, a thick, suffocating silence that seemed to press in from every corner. The air was heavy, laden with something unspoken.

"You've been here before," Eleanor blurted, unable to hold back the thought any longer. Her voice shook as she spoke, but she couldn't let the question fester unanswered. "You both—you—you've been here before. You're not strangers to this place, are you?"

The woman's lips twitched, a ghost of a smile appearing before it vanished as quickly as it came. The man, however, did not smile. His gaze remained fixed on her, impassive, unreadable.

"I've been here," the man said finally, his voice almost mechanical. "But that's not important. What matters now is that you understand the rules. The rules of this place."

"The rules?" Eleanor repeated, confused. "What do you mean?"

The woman stepped forward now, her movements smooth, almost unnerving in their precision. She raised one hand, as if to silence Eleanor's questions before they could gain any traction.

"You've crossed a line, Miss Westwood," she said softly. "A line that cannot be uncrossed. This place—this retreat—is not what you think it is. There are forces at work here, forces beyond your understanding. You will not be leaving until it is time."

A sharp gasp left Eleanor's lips. The cabin suddenly felt much smaller, the walls closing in. She stepped back instinctively, but the man's eyes followed her, tracking her every movement, his gaze like a weight pressing on her chest.

The woman's voice followed her, almost a whisper now, echoing in the silence.

"This is not a place of healing, Miss Westwood. Not for you. Not for anyone who comes seeking answers they're not prepared to face."

Eleanor could hardly breathe. The pieces were beginning to fall into place, but they didn't make any sense. This wasn't a retreat. It was a trap.

"Please," Eleanor said, her voice barely above a whisper. "I—I don't understand. What do you want from me?"

The woman's expression hardened, her lips thinning into a line. She didn't need to say anything. The atmosphere in the room had already shifted, a thick, suffocating tension hanging between them. Eleanor could feel the weight of it in her bones.

"We don't want anything from you," the woman said, her tone colder now. "But you, Miss Westwood, have already given something. Something important. Something we're going to make sure you never forget."

A chill ran down Eleanor's spine. She felt her legs begin to shake, but she steadied herself against the wall, her mind racing. What had she given? What did they want? Was this all part of some twisted game? She had come for solitude. She had come for peace.

But all she had found was this.

The man stepped forward then, his movements slow but deliberate. His presence seemed to fill the room, his towering form casting long shadows over her.

"Don't fight it," he said softly. "You're already a part of this place. Just as we are. Just as everyone who's come before you has been. You'll see. You'll understand."

Eleanor's blood ran cold. *Everyone who's come before me?*

Without another word, the man and the woman turned and moved toward the door. The woman glanced back over her shoulder, her dark eyes boring into Eleanor's soul.

"The night is far from over," she said, her voice like ice. "Rest while you can. Tomorrow, you will learn more."

Eleanor stood in the center of the room, her body trembling, her mind a whirlwind of confusion and fear. The fire crackled in the hearth, casting dancing shadows on the walls, but all she could hear was the deafening silence, the weight of the unknown pressing down on her like a suffocating fog.

And as the door closed behind the two figures, leaving her alone in the stillness of the cabin, Eleanor knew that nothing would ever be the same again.

She was trapped. Trapped in a story she didn't understand, and there was no way out.

4

Beneath the Surface

Eleanor woke in the early hours of the morning, the deep shadows of the cabin pressing down on her as she lay motionless in the bed. Her eyes fluttered open, but it took her several moments to orient herself. The remnants of a dream lingered at the edges of her mind—something fleeting, like a whisper just out of reach, but there was no mistaking the eerie sense of disconnection that clung to her like a heavy fog. Her body was still tired, drained from the strange encounter the night before, but her mind was sharp, buzzing with confusion.

She had to find answers. Now.

The cabin was colder than it had been when she fell asleep. The fire had died to a few glowing embers, their soft light barely illuminating the room. The wind outside was silent for the moment, but the distant howls from the forest seemed to reach inside the walls, chilling the very air. Eleanor's breath formed small clouds as she sat up, the covers slipping off her body to reveal a shiver running through her.

Her thoughts spun, trying to make sense of everything. The figures from last night—the man and the woman—were no longer in the cabin. She hadn't heard them leave, but their absence was unmistakable. Eleanor couldn't tell if they had been real or figments of her imagination, but the cold weight of their words, their presence, had been all too real. The woman's cryptic warning still echoed in her mind: You're already a part of this place.

The thought sent a jolt of panic through her chest. What did it mean? Why was she here, and what were they talking about? And that strange figure she had seen outside in the fog—was it the same man? Why had he been watching her?

Her hands trembled slightly as she slid off the bed and stepped onto the cold floor. Every movement felt unnatural, like she was intruding in someone else's world. She had to get out. Had to leave before it was too late, before whatever twisted game this was trapped her completely. But as soon as the thought formed, another part of her—the part that had been taught to trust her instincts—warned her that escaping wasn't an option. Not yet.

She crossed the small room quickly, pulling the curtains aside and peering out through the window. The morning light was weak, barely touching the surface of the mountainside, and the dense fog still clung to the trees like a shroud. She saw nothing unusual, no signs of the figures from last night, but that only made her more uneasy. There was no clear reason to be afraid, and yet, her heart hammered in her chest as if she was being hunted.

The cabin felt too quiet. Too still.

Turning away from the window, Eleanor approached the small table in the center of the room. A kettle sat on the edge, untouched from the previous night, and next to it, a worn map of the area. Her fingers traced the edges of the map without thinking, the delicate lines of the roads and trails barely visible beneath the faint smudges of age.

As her hand brushed over it, something peculiar caught her attention. The map wasn't exactly right. She had seen this area before, but some of the landmarks seemed... wrong. The lake, the one she was supposedly near, didn't match the layout she remembered from the pamphlet she had received when booking the retreat. There were discrepancies in the paths marked and places that shouldn't exist—places that weren't on the brochures. She frowned, turning the map sideways to better read the faded symbols and lines, but the more she studied it, the more confusing it became.

Had someone altered it deliberately? Was this another sign that she was not meant to be here?

Her fingers lingered over a circle drawn in thick red ink near the edge of the map. The circle was surrounding something called "The Hollow." There was no description, no clue as to what this place was, but the name alone sent a ripple of unease through her.

She needed answers.

There was a knock on the door. Soft at first, but then louder, insistent.

Eleanor jumped, her heart leaping in her chest as she hurried to the door, wiping her sweaty palms on her jeans. Her mind raced with the possibilities. Was it the man and woman? Had they returned? She couldn't bring herself to turn the handle immediately. Fear gnawed at her insides, and the rational part of her knew she should at least try to talk to them. But what could she say?

Opening the door slightly, she peered out into the gray morning. A figure stood at the threshold, but it wasn't the man or the woman. It was another person. A man, younger than the other two, dressed in the same dark clothes as they had been, though his face was not nearly as hard or intimidating. His expression was somewhat nervous, and his eyes darted from side to side as if making sure no one else was watching.

"Miss Westwood," he said, his voice low and hesitant. "I need to speak with you."

Eleanor froze. She didn't know this man, and yet his presence seemed just as ominous as the others. "Who are you?" she asked, her voice shaky, though she tried to sound confident.

"My name is Theo," he replied, stepping slightly closer, but not too close, as though respecting some invisible boundary. "I'm... I'm not like them." He motioned to the cabin behind him. "I don't want to be here either."

Eleanor's mind raced. What does he mean, 'not like them'? She took a step back, instinctively pulling the door closed behind her. She didn't know whether she should be afraid or relieved.

"I don't understand," Eleanor said, swallowing her fear. "What's going on here? Why is this place so... strange?"

Theo glanced around again, his face twitching with anxiety. He seemed to be debating something in his head before he spoke again, voice barely above a whisper.

"I think I can explain," he said. "But not here. Not like this. It's too dangerous."

"Dangerous?" Eleanor repeated. She didn't trust him, but part of her—a small part—believed him. There was an honesty in his eyes that the others lacked. "What's dangerous about it?"

He hesitated again, clearly struggling to find the right words. "The Hollow. It's more than just a place. It's... it's a part of the land itself. A place that, once it has you, doesn't let go. No one really comes back from it."

A cold shiver crawled up Eleanor's spine. "But I—I didn't mean to—"

"You didn't mean to," Theo cut in quickly, "but you've already crossed over. You're part of this now. The moment you stepped onto this land, you became part of the story."

Eleanor's throat went dry. She wanted to scream, to demand

to know more, but all she could manage was a weak nod.

"Please," Theo urged, his voice almost desperate now. "Come with me. You have to see it for yourself. You need to know what you're really up against."

Eleanor stood there, caught between the growing storm of fear and the odd urge to trust Theo. He had seemed out of place from the moment she laid eyes on him, and yet, there was something compelling about his vulnerability, about the way he spoke as if he, too, were trapped in this nightmare.

She glanced back into the cabin, the oppressive silence looming over her. The woman's words echoed in her mind: Rest while you can. Tomorrow, you will learn more.

But tomorrow? Tomorrow might be too late.

"What happens if I don't go with you?" Eleanor asked, her voice tight.

Theo's face darkened, and his gaze dropped to the ground for a moment before meeting her eyes again. "You don't want to find out."

For a moment, Eleanor felt the weight of the decision press down on her chest, suffocating her. She had no choice. She had to know the truth, no matter how terrifying it might be.

Without another word, she stepped out of the cabin, her heart pounding as the door clicked shut behind her. She didn't know where this path would lead, but in that moment, Eleanor understood one thing above all else: there was no turning back.

The Hollow was waiting. And it was already too late to escape.

5

Through the Mist

Eleanor's heart beat heavily in her chest as she stepped outside into the fog that had swallowed the cabin. It clung to her skin, damp and oppressive, as if the air itself was trying to drag her back into the shadows. The ground beneath her feet was soft with wet moss, and the faint smell of decay hung in the stillness. The path ahead of her was barely visible through the thickening mist, winding its way through the dense trees, their gnarled branches reaching like skeletal hands.

Theo stood just a few feet away, his back to her, hands shoved deep into the pockets of his coat. He was waiting for her to make up her mind. The decision had already been made, though, the moment he'd spoken about The Hollow. Eleanor's mind raced, churning with confusion and fear, but the chill in the air—both from the landscape and his words—made her move forward. She couldn't afford to hesitate any longer.

Theo didn't look back as he started walking. His footsteps were muted against the moss-covered ground, but the silence between them was deafening, filled with the weight of unsaid words and unseen dangers.

Eleanor followed, keeping a few steps behind. The fog parted slightly ahead of her, but not enough to reveal anything beyond the twisted trees and thick undergrowth. The further they walked, the more unnatural it felt—like they were leaving the realm of the living behind and stepping into something else. The air grew colder with every step, and the light from the weak morning sun filtered down in diffused beams that hardly seemed to touch the earth.

After several minutes of walking in silence, Theo spoke, his voice low and hesitant. "You're probably wondering why I'm here. Why I stayed."

Eleanor didn't reply, but she couldn't stop herself from glancing over at him. He was tall, his features sharp, and despite the eerie quiet around them, there was an unshakable sincerity in his expression. She didn't trust him completely, but she didn't sense any malice, either. Not like the others.

"You're not the first one to come here," Theo continued, eyes scanning the path ahead as if the fog itself held secrets. "This land... it takes people. Slowly. At first, it just makes you question things. You think you're imagining stuff. Then, it gets worse."

"Worse?" Eleanor echoed, a knot forming in her stomach. She had an inkling of what he meant, but hearing it out loud made it more real, more terrifying.

Theo stopped walking, turning to face her, his expression now dark, his eyes shadowed by something unspeakable. The forest around them seemed to grow still, as though even the trees were waiting for his words.

"You're here because of the retreat," he said, his voice barely a whisper. "Because you thought it was a place to heal. But no one leaves The Hollow healed. No one."

Eleanor's throat tightened, her pulse quickening. The Hollow. The name had been whispered in her mind since she'd seen it on the map, but hearing it from Theo, hearing the gravity in his voice, made it feel all too real.

"What is The Hollow?" she demanded, her voice sharp despite the fear gnawing at her. "And why does it... take people?"

Theo's gaze flickered, and he lowered his head for a moment, almost as if he was ashamed. "The Hollow isn't just a place. It's a part of this land. A curse, maybe. Something older than all of us. Those who come here... they don't just leave behind their pasts. They leave behind pieces of themselves. Pieces that get absorbed by the land. That's how it survives."

Eleanor's breath hitched as she tried to digest his words. Pieces of themselves? Was he talking about souls? She couldn't make sense of it.

Before she could ask another question, Theo turned and began walking again, faster this time, as if the shadows at his back were closing in.

"Come on," he urged. "We have to keep moving."

Eleanor followed, a growing sense of urgency propelling her forward. The mist had thickened, curling around her like an oppressive blanket. The trees, their trunks twisted and bent in unnatural shapes, seemed to close in on them, narrowing the path with every step. The air was becoming harder to breathe, as though it was thick with something unseen—something that made the world feel off-kilter.

Theo's footsteps grew quicker, more frantic, and Eleanor found herself struggling to keep pace. Her breath was coming faster now, sharp and cold, her heart racing. She felt the prickle of sweat on the back of her neck, and a cold dread spread through her chest.

"What's happening?" she gasped, her voice rising in panic. "Why are we running?"

Theo didn't answer right away. He just kept moving, faster, more determined, until the path before them split into two— one trail leading off to the left, the other continuing straight ahead into the thickest part of the trees. He veered left, almost as if he'd memorized the way. Eleanor's mind raced, but there was no time for doubt. She followed him, her eyes scanning the mist for any sign of danger.

The silence of the forest was suddenly broken by a faint, eerie whisper, coming from somewhere in the distance. It was a low, haunting sound that seemed to float on the air, tugging at her thoughts like a distant call.

"What is that?" Eleanor breathed, her voice barely above a whisper.

Theo's eyes were wide now, his face pale. He didn't answer, but the fear in his gaze was enough to tell her everything she needed to know.

"Run!" he shouted suddenly, his voice cracking with urgency.

Eleanor didn't hesitate. She ran, her feet pounding against the soft earth, her heart hammering in her chest. The fog was so thick now that she could barely see her own hands in front of her. The sound of Theo's footsteps grew more frantic, more desperate, until they seemed to fade altogether. She called his name, but the mist swallowed her voice, leaving her in a suffocating silence.

Then she heard it.

A soft rustling behind her, followed by a low, guttural growl. Eleanor's blood turned to ice. Something was moving in the fog. Something large. Something close.

She turned, her breath catching in her throat, but saw nothing. Just the dense, swirling mist. Her pulse thundered in her ears as she pushed forward, faster now, her mind barely able to grasp what was happening. The path before her seemed to stretch on forever, twisting and turning as if the forest itself was conspiring against her.

Then, she saw it—a shadow moving in the mist, too large to be human. It was tall, towering over her, and its presence seemed to block out the very light of the fog. The growl came again, this time much closer. Eleanor's instincts screamed at her to run, but her legs felt like lead. Fear had a grip on her so tight she couldn't breathe.

The shadow moved again, and Eleanor's blood ran cold. It wasn't just the size of the figure that terrified her—it was the way it seemed to flicker in and out of existence, like a mirage that couldn't decide if it was real or not.

Suddenly, Theo appeared before her, his face a mask of terror. "Run!" he shouted again, grabbing her arm and pulling her toward him.

He didn't need to say it twice. Eleanor ran, this time with every ounce of strength she had left. Her breath came in ragged gasps, her vision blurry as she tried to focus on the path ahead of her. The growls grew louder, closer, and for the first time in her life, Eleanor knew what true terror felt like.

They ran for what felt like an eternity, the mist swirling around them, choking out everything in its path. The world had turned into a nightmare, a place that defied reason, where reality had begun to fracture and bend.

And then, just as Eleanor thought she couldn't go any further, the fog suddenly cleared. The trees parted, and before them stood a clearing—a vast, open space that stretched out before her, a landscape she couldn't recognize. It was cold, barren, the earth cracked and dry, like the aftermath of some great catastrophe.

In the center of the clearing stood a stone structure, ancient and weathered, its surface covered in strange symbols that seemed to pulse with a faint, otherworldly light. The Hollow.

Eleanor's breath caught in her throat. This was it. This was where it began. And in that moment, she realized something that chilled her to the bone: The Hollow was not just a place. It was a trap. And now, there was no way out.

6

The Eyes Beneath the Stone

The air inside the clearing was heavier than before, laden with a scent that was both metallic and earthy. Eleanor's chest tightened as she took a few steps forward, the ground beneath her feet unnervingly solid, like it was made of ancient stone, though the rest of the forest had been soft with moss and damp earth. She could feel a strange vibration in her bones, as though the very land was alive and watching her.

Theo had fallen silent beside her, his steps now slow, deliberate. The wild panic that had gripped him before had faded into a tense quiet, as if something had commanded his obedience. Eleanor tried to catch her breath, her pulse hammering in her throat. She could still hear the distant growls, faint but undeniable—somewhere behind the mist, something was moving, and it was getting closer. Yet, here they were, in the middle of an open space, with no sign of life but the eerie silence around them.

The stone structure in front of them loomed like a monument to some forgotten god, its surface etched with symbols that defied recognition. The markings twisted and spiraled in patterns that made Eleanor's head spin as she tried to decipher them, but each attempt only deepened her sense of unease. The structure seemed ancient, as though it had stood there for centuries—no, for millennia—waiting for them to come. And yet, despite its age, there was something unsettlingly new about it, as if it had just been waiting for the right moment to reveal itself.

Eleanor's gaze moved upward, scanning the structure for any clue as to its purpose, but all she could see were the symbols—runes, perhaps—intertwining in ways that made no sense. Her mind raced as she tried to make sense of the scene, but it was as though everything around her was intentionally designed to confuse, to make her doubt her own senses.

Theo took another step forward, his face drawn with fear. "It's calling to us," he muttered, as though speaking more to himself than to her. "The Hollow always calls. And once you hear it, you can never stop listening."

Eleanor stared at him, her mind still reeling from his last words. "What do you mean? What is this place?"

Theo's lips parted as though he was about to speak, but the words seemed stuck in his throat. He clenched his fists at his sides, as if battling some invisible force that was preventing him from answering.

Then, a loud crack echoed through the clearing.

Eleanor spun around, her heart leaping into her throat. The fog had shifted again, coiling inwards, as if something was moving just beyond her vision. The growl she had heard earlier returned, louder now, almost deafening. But this time, it was not a distant rumble. It was close. Too close.

The air grew colder, impossibly so, and Eleanor's breath came in sharp bursts. She could feel the hairs on the back of her neck stand on end, her instincts screaming at her to run, to escape this place while she still could. But there was nowhere to run. The clearing was surrounded by the mist, and beyond that—the Hollow.

"Run!" Theo shouted suddenly, his voice breaking the tension, and he grabbed her arm, pulling her toward the stone structure.

Eleanor barely had time to react before the growl came again, a low, guttural sound that seemed to come from all around them. The ground beneath her feet trembled, and she stumbled, nearly losing her balance as Theo dragged her along. She didn't have to look back to know what was behind them—she could feel it, a presence growing closer, wrapping around them like a noose.

The stone structure loomed ahead, impossibly large now that they were so close. It seemed to have grown taller in the few seconds they'd been moving toward it. The symbols on its surface were no longer just markings. They were moving. Alive.

Eleanor's breath caught in her throat as she watched the runes shift before her eyes. They spiraled inward, merging and twisting, converging on the center of the stone like a vortex. And then, just as she thought she couldn't take it anymore, the structure seemed to breathe—shuddering as if it had been waiting for them all along.

Theo pushed her forward, his grip tight on her arm. "We have to get inside," he urged, his voice frantic. "The Hollow doesn't let you leave. Not once you've heard it. Not once you've crossed its threshold."

Eleanor's mind was racing, her thoughts a whirlwind of questions and dread, but she didn't hesitate. She couldn't. Not with the growl growing louder behind them, with the ground beneath them shaking, and the strange hum of energy that filled the air. She didn't understand what was happening, but she knew one thing for sure: she had to go with Theo. There was no other choice.

The stone doors of the structure swung open as they approached, groaning on ancient hinges. A dark, inky shadow waited beyond, deep and suffocating. Eleanor hesitated only for a moment, the fear gnawing at her insides, before Theo pushed her inside. She stumbled, catching herself against the cold stone walls as she entered.

The door slammed shut behind them with a deafening finality.

Inside, the temperature dropped even further, and Eleanor gasped as she found herself in a vast chamber. The walls were smooth, almost too smooth, and they seemed to stretch up forever into the darkness. She couldn't see the ceiling, just an endless void above them. There were no windows, no openings—just stone and more stone. It felt like they had stepped into the belly of something ancient, something that had been buried for centuries.

The air was thick with an unidentifiable scent, both sour and sweet, and as they moved deeper into the chamber, Eleanor noticed strange markings on the floor—circles, symbols, runes that pulsed faintly with a greenish light.

Theo was already moving toward a narrow passageway at the far end of the room, his footsteps quick and purposeful. Eleanor followed, unsure of what was pulling her along—whether it was the fear that clung to her or the sense that, if she didn't, she might be lost forever.

As they passed the symbols, they seemed to shift, almost imperceptibly, as if they were watching her, judging her. The sensation was unnerving, but Eleanor couldn't stop now. She couldn't think, couldn't process the madness around her. She just had to keep moving.

Theo reached the narrow passage and paused, turning to look at her with a haunted expression. "You have to understand," he said, his voice barely more than a whisper. "Once you've come this far, there's no going back. The Hollow doesn't let you leave. Ever."

Eleanor swallowed, her mouth dry. "What are you talking about? What is this place? Why are we here?"

Theo's face seemed to collapse under the weight of his words. "It's too late for me. But you... you might still have a chance."

Eleanor's heart skipped a beat. "A chance? A chance at what?"

He didn't answer immediately. Instead, he stepped back into the passageway, and for the first time, Eleanor saw a glimmer of something in his eyes—a spark of hope, mingled with fear. "The Hollow gives you a choice. But you have to be willing to face it. The truth is in there, but you have to be willing to walk through the darkness to find it. Otherwise..."

Eleanor stepped forward, reaching for him. "Otherwise, what?"

Theo hesitated, his lips trembling. "Otherwise, the Hollow takes everything."

Before she could react, he turned and disappeared into the darkness, swallowed by the shadows of the narrow passage.

Eleanor stood frozen, her mind racing. She didn't know what was real anymore. The growls, the symbols, the whispers—it was all a blur. But one thing was clear: The Hollow had chosen her.

And now, she was trapped.

7

The Depths of Desire

Eleanor's breath was shallow as she stood in the darkness, her pulse thrumming in her ears. The silence of the narrow passageway seemed to close in around her, a dense, suffocating presence that threatened to crush her. She could barely see beyond the dim light that flickered from the strange greenish symbols on the walls. They pulsed like a heartbeat, their glow weak but constant, casting long, eerie shadows that seemed to slither along the stone floor.

Theo's words echoed in her mind: The Hollow takes everything. Her stomach churned, and her chest tightened as a wave of dread washed over her. She didn't understand. None of this made sense. The Hollow? The curse? The land? It was too much, too overwhelming, and yet, she couldn't shake the feeling that there was something deeper waiting for her—something she had to confront, no matter how terrifying.

Her hands shook as she reached out to steady herself against the cold stone of the wall. The chill that radiated from the surface seeped into her skin, numbing her fingertips as though the very walls were alive, hungry, and thirsty for warmth. Her legs felt weak, but there was no turning back now. Theo was ahead of her—she didn't know how far—and she had to find him, or whatever it was that had lured him into this dark, inescapable place.

Taking a deep breath, Eleanor stepped forward, the soft crunch of her boots the only sound in the silence. She tried not to think about the growls, the ominous vibrations in the air, or the feeling that she was being drawn into something that had been waiting for centuries. Instead, she focused on the narrow passage ahead, the faint flicker of green light that promised some semblance of direction.

The tunnel twisted and turned as she walked, the walls narrowing until they felt as though they might crush her. She could hear her heartbeat in her ears now, faster and faster as her anxiety grew. There was no telling how far this path stretched, how deep the Hollow really went. The light in front of her seemed to grow fainter the farther she went, until it was just a distant glow, teasing her with its unreachable promise. The air grew heavier with every step, thick with an unseen presence.

Suddenly, the path opened up.

Eleanor stumbled into a wide cavern, her eyes widening as she took in the sight before her. It was like stepping into another world—a place untouched by time, yet older than anything she could comprehend. The cavern was vast, its ceiling lost in shadow, but the walls were lined with stone carvings that stretched from floor to ceiling. These weren't the twisting runes from the passageway. These were different—more intricate, more deliberate, and they seemed to tell a story.

At first, Eleanor couldn't make sense of them. They were filled with strange symbols, figures that resembled humans, but distorted in ways that made her blood run cold. Eyes that were too large, faces that were half-hidden, and limbs that twisted unnaturally. The figures were positioned in what seemed like a ritualistic dance, their arms outstretched, their hands reaching for something just beyond their grasp. She tried to focus on one image, but the longer she stared, the more it seemed to shift and change, the figures becoming blurred and indistinct, as though they were alive and moving in the shadows.

But it wasn't the carvings that caught Eleanor's attention. It was the center of the cavern. A large stone slab, resting on an altar of similar stone, bathed in an eerie glow that emanated from the walls. It looked ancient, its surface cracked and worn, but it radiated an undeniable power.

The moment she saw it, Eleanor knew that this was where she was supposed to be. A magnetic pull drew her toward it, and despite every instinct telling her to turn and run, she found herself moving forward.

Her heart raced as she stepped closer, her breath coming in ragged bursts. She had the strangest sensation of being watched—like hundreds of eyes were on her, tracking her every movement. But when she turned, there was nothing but stone, dark shadows, and the pulse of the strange glow that illuminated the slab.

Reaching the altar, Eleanor's fingers hovered just above its surface, the air thick with anticipation. She could feel the weight of it, like the stone itself was waiting for her to touch it. She didn't know what would happen if she did—whether she would be swallowed up by the darkness, or if the Hollow would finally claim her. But she couldn't stop herself.

Her hand made contact.

A shockwave of cold energy rippled through her body, and for a moment, everything went white. The ground seemed to tremble beneath her feet, and her heart stuttered in her chest as an overwhelming wave of emotion crashed over her. It was like a flood, a torrent of images and sensations that slammed into her mind all at once.

Faces, voices, memories—not her own, but of those who had come before her. She saw them clearly, as if they were standing right in front of her. Some were smiling, others crying, their faces twisted in fear or joy. The images blurred into each other, swirling like water, until one face emerged from the chaos.

Theo.

Her heart clenched, and she tried to pull back, but her hand remained stuck to the slab, the cold energy now racing through her veins, filling her body with a strange power. It was as though she was connected to something far greater than herself—something ancient, something alive. The ground beneath her shifted, and the images of the faces began to solidify, focusing on Theo's.

His eyes were wide, desperate, as though he were trapped inside a dream he couldn't escape.

Eleanor tried to speak, to call out to him, but no sound escaped her lips. She wanted to scream, to warn him, but the words were stuck in her throat, just as they had been when she first touched the stone.

Then, in a sudden flash, the vision changed.

Theo's face morphed, his features contorting into something unrecognizable. His eyes turned black, devoid of light, and his mouth stretched into a twisted grin. His voice—low and guttural—whispered in her ear.

"You shouldn't have come, Eleanor. No one ever leaves The Hollow."

The words pierced through her, and the flood of visions stopped as suddenly as it had begun. The cavern fell silent. The eerie glow from the stone slab dimmed, and the weight that had pressed down on her seemed to lift. But Eleanor's hand was still glued to the stone. She tried to pull away, but the energy had her trapped, its cold grip unyielding.

Her pulse was pounding in her ears, but now, she wasn't sure if it was fear or something else—something far deeper. The deeper she probed, the more she felt it pulling her in. It was like the Hollow itself was alive, feeding off her confusion and fear, taking hold of her in ways she couldn't understand.

"Please," Eleanor whispered, her voice trembling. "Let me go."

But the stone slab seemed to pulse in answer, its rhythm matching the frantic beat of her heart. A low hum vibrated in the air, a resonance that she felt deep within her bones. It wasn't just a sound. It was calling to her, beckoning her to stay.

Then, in the silence that followed, she heard it—a voice, barely audible, as if it came from the very stone itself.

Choose.

Her breath caught in her throat. The voice was so soft, so gentle, that for a moment, she wasn't sure if she had imagined it. But then it came again, clearer this time.

Choose. Or be lost forever.

The walls of the cavern began to shift again, the shadows creeping along the stone, lengthening and twisting like tendrils of smoke. Eleanor's heart raced. She wanted to run, to flee, but there was nowhere to go. She had entered this place with a sense of purpose, with the hope of understanding, but now, that purpose felt like a lie.

The voice continued, its tone almost sad, but compelling.

Choose, Eleanor. Choose or be consumed.

Terror gripped her as the weight of the choice pressed down on her, but she couldn't see the way forward. She didn't know what she was choosing. Was it her life? Her soul? Or something more sinister?

Eleanor's mind raced as the shadows grew, reaching out to her with ghostly fingers. The Hollow had her now. The only question was whether she could escape its grasp—or if it would devour her completely.

8

The Shattered Path

The air around Eleanor felt heavy, suffused with a palpable dread that seemed to twist her insides. Every breath she took was shallow, as though the cavern itself was closing in on her chest, squeezing the life from her. The hum that had filled the space before—so soft, so insistent—had now turned into a steady thrum, reverberating in her skull. It felt as though it was coming from the stone, or perhaps from the earth itself. A pulse. A heartbeat. A warning.

She tried to pull her hand away from the stone, but it was as if her skin had fused with it, her fingers locked into place by an invisible force that refused to let go. The cold of the stone had seeped deep into her bones, a frost that no warmth could melt. Her pulse thrummed in rhythm with the strange hum around her, her mind filled with images—visions—that she couldn't quite grasp. Faces she'd never seen before. People she couldn't name. Their eyes were empty. Their mouths were wide, as though they were screaming, but no sound reached her ears.

"Please... let me go..." she whispered, though she knew the words would have no meaning. Nothing here obeyed words.

The voice from the stone—the one that had echoed through her soul—spoke again, its tone soft, coaxing.

Choose.

Her heart skipped a beat, the familiar voice seeming to press on her mind, curling its fingers around her thoughts like tendrils of smoke. The word echoed within her, reverberating in her very core.

Choose or be lost.

The ground beneath her feet trembled, and the stone altar shuddered with a terrible force. Eleanor's head swam, her thoughts dissolving into confusion as the thrum of the stone grew louder, deeper. It wasn't just a sound now; it was a feeling—a pull. A magnetic force that reached deep into her chest, tugging her forward. She wanted to tear her hand away, to run, to scream, but the force holding her there was relentless, unyielding.

Behind her, the passageway to the cavern had closed, a solid wall of stone where the path had once been. No escape. Only the altar, the stone, and the growing darkness that pressed on every side. The walls of the cavern seemed to be narrowing, the shadows creeping toward her as if the very air was closing in.

Eleanor's breath hitched. "Choose what?" she called out to the darkness, her voice trembling. "What do you want from me?"

The hum ceased. Silence fell, heavy and suffocating.

Then, in the stillness, the voice returned—this time, it was different. Deeper. More insistent.

You must choose who you will become.

The words resonated within her, filling her mind with a thousand unanswered questions. Who would she become? What was the Hollow? What was this place? This entity? What had Theo meant when he spoke of the Hollow taking everything?

Eleanor looked down at her hand, still pressed to the stone. The symbols on the altar had shifted—changed—like they were alive, writhing beneath her palm. They twisted and undulated, drawing shapes that reminded her of faces, of people she had known, and people she had not. The runes stretched and reformed, forming images that seemed to call to her, beckoning her deeper into their mysteries.

It was as if the stone was trying to show her something, something important—something she needed to understand, but the more she focused on the images, the more her mind slipped away from them. The darkness in the cavern seemed to grow, swallowing the light. She could feel the weight of it, pressing against her, pushing at the edges of her mind.

Choose.

Eleanor closed her eyes tightly, trying to block out the pulse, the pressure, the all-consuming sense that something was about to break. She felt her hand begin to tingle, an intense warmth spreading up her arm from where it touched the stone, as if the cold was being drawn out of her, leaving something new in its place. Her skin prickled, and she gasped, pulling her hand away, but the warmth continued to burn in her palm, radiating through her body like fire.

And then, as though the stone had taken everything—her fear, her breath, her strength—it spoke once more.

You have already made your choice.

Eleanor's eyes snapped open, her heart pounding in her chest. She tried to speak, but her voice caught in her throat. Something had shifted. She could feel it in the very marrow of her bones. A sudden realization flooded through her like a torrent. She had made her choice. It had already been made, long before she had even stepped into this place.

But what choice? And what had she agreed to?

The symbols on the stone flared to life in front of her, glowing brighter now, burning with an intensity that was almost blinding. For a moment, Eleanor was frozen—her entire body locked in place, her heart racing, her thoughts scattering. The cavern was spinning, the walls warping and distorting, as though the very world around her was breaking apart.

And then, she saw him.

Theo.

He was standing in the center of the altar, his face pale, his eyes wide with terror. His hands were raised in front of him, palms outstretched, as though trying to keep something at bay. But there was nothing around him. Nothing to keep at arm's length except the dark, suffocating space. The walls of the cavern seemed to breathe, drawing in closer, as though the very air was alive, and it was alive with fear.

"Eleanor..." Theo's voice broke through the madness, weak, desperate. "It's not what you think. It's not—"

Before he could finish, the shadows around him seemed to bend, twisting and spiraling, closing in like an engulfing flood. Eleanor reached out toward him instinctively, but the moment her fingers brushed the air, the space between them crackled with an electric charge that threw her back. She stumbled, barely catching herself on the edge of the stone altar.

Theo's body began to fade. His form blurred, his features melting away into the blackness, his voice turning into a hollow scream that echoed through the cavern, bouncing off the walls like a dying whisper. The shadows engulfed him completely, and for a split second, Eleanor could feel the pull of the stone, the power surging through the ground beneath her feet.

And then, he was gone.

The silence that followed was worse than the growls she had heard earlier, worse than the hum of the stone. It was an emptiness, a hollow, aching void. She could still hear the remnants of his voice in her head—still feel the echoes of his fear.

She sank to her knees, her hands trembling, her mind reeling. What had happened? What had the Hollow taken from him? What had it taken from her?

The voice in her mind—soft, whispering—spoke again.

Everything is a choice.

Eleanor's breath hitched in her throat. What did that mean? Was the Hollow manipulating her, feeding off her fears? Or had she been tricked into making a choice she didn't even understand?

She looked down at her hands, her fingertips raw from the stone, and then her eyes wandered back to the altar. The runes had gone dark again, the light fading as if it had been snuffed out. The cavern had returned to its former state, the shadows curling and shifting, but they no longer felt alive. The pulse, the hum—everything was gone. The air felt still, dead.

Except for one thing.

A faint sound echoed through the darkness—soft, barely audible, like the sound of something scraping against stone.

Eleanor's head snapped toward the sound, her heart racing. The passageway behind her—the one that had been closed off when she had first touched the stone—was slowly, imperceptibly, opening.

And at the threshold of the passage stood something, or rather, someone.

Eleanor's breath caught in her throat as the figure stepped forward into the dim light. His face was shadowed, but she recognized him instantly.

Theo.

But it wasn't the Theo she had known. His eyes were black, empty, and his mouth stretched into a grin that was far too wide.

The Hollow never lets you leave, he whispered, his voice low and rasping. And neither will you.

Eleanor's body froze. The truth—the full, horrific truth—was dawning on her. She wasn't trapped in the Hollow.

She was becoming part of it.

The path she had walked to get here? Shattered. Forever gone. She had entered this place, thinking she could choose. But the Hollow had made her its own.

And now, it had claimed her.

The shadows reached for her, and Eleanor knew, with a sinking certainty, that she was no longer alone.

9

The Echoes of Betrayal

Eleanor could feel the air thicken with a presence that was both oppressive and suffocating. The cavern around her, once vast and open, now felt as though the walls were closing in. The shadows stretched further, wrapping themselves around her like dark, whispering tendrils, pulling her closer to the heart of the Hollow. The stone altar loomed in front of her, its surface cold and alien, as though it were waiting for her to make the next move.

But she was no longer sure what to do. The voice that had once spoken to her so clearly, that had echoed through her mind with the promise of choice, had fallen silent. Now, there was only the weight of the darkness pressing down on her, the oppressive quiet broken only by the soft sound of her own breath and the distant scraping of the figure in the shadows.

Theo stood just at the edge of the passage, his body like a silhouette in the low light. His face was obscured by the shadows, but Eleanor could feel the intensity of his gaze. His eyes, black as night, seemed to burn through the air between them. The air crackled with tension, the silence so thick that it almost had a sound of its own—a deep, resonating hum that reverberated through her body.

For a moment, neither of them moved. It was as though the very space between them had frozen, trapping them both in a strange, timeless moment. Eleanor could barely breathe, her chest tight with a mixture of fear and confusion. Her mind raced, trying to make sense of what was happening, but it was all slipping away, like sand through her fingers.

"What happened to you?" she managed to whisper, her voice barely audible over the suffocating silence. She wasn't sure if she was speaking to Theo, to the Hollow, or to herself. She wasn't sure who she could trust anymore.

Theo's lips curled into a slow, twisted grin. The smile was wrong—unnatural. There was no warmth in it, no recognition. His features were sharper now, his face more gaunt, as though something had hollowed him out. It was as though the very essence of who he had been had been consumed by the Hollow. But still, she could feel him there—somewhere beneath the changes, beneath the corruption.

"You don't understand, Eleanor," he said, his voice low and gravely, like the sound of rocks scraping together. "You never did."

Her heart skipped a beat. The words echoed in her mind, sending a shiver down her spine. She had never understood?

The realization hit her like a bolt of lightning. She had been so caught up in her search for him, in her desire to save him, that she had never truly understood him—never truly understood what he had been running from.

A flash of memories surfaced, images of their time together before they had come to this place. Their laughter in the park, the quiet walks by the river, the soft way his hand had brushed against hers. It all seemed so distant now, so far removed from the cold figure before her. She had thought she knew him—had thought she understood his fears, his darkness. But this? This wasn't Theo. Not anymore.

"What happened to you?" she asked again, her voice shaking with a mixture of fear and desperation. "Why are you doing this?"

Theo stepped closer, his movements slow, deliberate. With each step, the shadows seemed to grow longer, stretching out in his wake like hungry fingers. As he neared, the temperature dropped, the air turning cold and biting. Eleanor shivered, instinctively stepping back. But there was nowhere to go. The cavern was closing in on her, the stone walls pressing in from all sides. The shadows followed her every movement, like they were alive—like they were watching her.

"You don't get it, do you?" Theo's voice was almost a whisper now, but it was sharp, cutting through the air. "The Hollow doesn't take—it transforms." He paused, his eyes burning with an intensity that sent a jolt of terror through her. "I was weak. You were weak. We were both weak. But now we're strong."

Eleanor's breath caught in her throat. "Strong?" she repeated, the word tasting bitter on her tongue. "What do you mean? This isn't strength. It's... it's wrong."

Theo's laugh echoed through the cavern, a low, rumbling sound that didn't belong to him. The sound of it made her stomach twist, like she had just swallowed something cold and foreign. He was no longer the man she had known—the man she had loved. Whatever he had become, it was something monstrous. The Hollow had corrupted him, twisted his mind and soul, until there was nothing left but a hollow shell of the person he had once been.

"You never understood, Eleanor," Theo said, his voice now like a growl. "You always believed that you could escape it, that you could save me. But this place isn't about saving. It's about becoming. It's about embracing the darkness, letting it fill you, letting it make you whole. That's what the Hollow offers— power."

Eleanor's legs shook beneath her, her body trembling with the force of the words, the weight of the revelation. Power? Was that what this was all about? Was this what Theo had been after all along? Was this why he had led her here, to this cursed place? Had he known from the beginning that there was no way out—that this was his destiny, his fate?

"No," she whispered, the word escaping her lips before she could stop it. "I won't become like you. I won't let the Hollow take me."

Theo's eyes flickered with something like amusement, as if her words were nothing more than a passing distraction. He tilted his head, regarding her with a look that was both sad and contemptuous. "You're already here, Eleanor. You've already made your choice. You just don't realize it yet."

The air around her seemed to grow heavier, pressing in on her from all sides, suffocating her. She could feel the weight of his words sinking into her, worming their way into her mind. Had she already made her choice? Had she already sealed her fate when she stepped into the Hollow? Was this place truly inescapable?

The ground beneath her feet trembled, and she stumbled, her hand reaching out to steady herself against the altar. Her breath was shallow, her heart hammering in her chest. She couldn't breathe. She couldn't think. The shadows seemed to press in on her, pulling her toward the darkness.

Theo reached out, his fingers brushing against her arm, sending a jolt of cold through her body. "You'll see soon enough, Eleanor," he said, his voice soft and cruel. "This is who we are now. There's no going back. There's only forward. Only the Hollow."

Her mind reeled. She couldn't believe what he was saying. She couldn't accept it. She had to fight. She had to find a way out.

But as Theo's grip tightened, the shadows around them began to shift, moving like a living thing, crawling across the walls and the floor. The cavern seemed to shift with them, the walls warping and twisting, stretching until they became unrecognizable. The shadows seemed to have a life of their own, swirling together in a vortex of darkness, and Eleanor felt herself being pulled toward it, helpless.

No. She couldn't give in. She wouldn't.

"Let go of me!" she shouted, her voice raw with panic. She tried to wrench herself free from Theo's grasp, but his fingers dug into her skin, unyielding. The power in his touch was suffocating, draining the strength from her.

"You'll understand soon enough," Theo said, his voice distant, as though he were no longer speaking to her at all. "The Hollow doesn't let go. Not of us. Not of anyone."

The shadows swirled around them, pulling them closer to the heart of the cavern. Eleanor could feel the cold, the deep, suffocating darkness that was consuming everything in its path. The walls seemed to pulse with a strange energy, thrumming with an ancient power that she couldn't comprehend. The ground shook, and she could hear the faintest whisper—a voice from deep within the shadows.

Choose.

The word echoed in her mind, louder than before, like a cry, like a command. It wasn't the same voice from before. It was different now. Deeper. More forceful. And yet, it was the same, the same presence that had been with her since the beginning. It was the Hollow. It was calling her.

Eleanor's heart raced. She could feel the weight of the choice before her, pressing on her chest, suffocating her. She didn't know what to choose. She didn't know what was real anymore. But one thing was certain: the Hollow had already taken so much from her. And Theo—Theo was lost.

But her will wasn't.

"I won't let you take me!" she cried, the words coming from deep within her, as though they were fueled by every ounce of resistance she had left.

For a moment, everything stopped. The shadows stilled. The thrum of power faded. And in that brief silence, Eleanor felt a flicker of something inside her—something small but fierce.

She wasn't going to let the Hollow consume her.

Not yet. Not ever.

Her heart thundered in her chest as she shoved Theo's hand away, the raw strength of her defiance momentarily breaking through the darkness. And in that moment, the cavern seemed

to hold its breath, waiting for her next move.

10

The Whispering Depths

The cold burned through Eleanor's skin as though the shadows themselves had turned to ice, piercing her body with a sharpness she hadn't known was possible. She could feel the weight of it, the pressure of the cavern itself, as though the very stone and earth beneath her feet were holding her captive, unwilling to let her escape. Theo's grip on her arm, though momentarily loosened, still lingered, like a chill that had settled deep within her bones. She could feel his presence at her side, his eyes boring into her with an intensity that was both haunting and suffocating. She was still trapped, locked in the heart of this forsaken place, with no way out—yet.

Her breath was ragged, her heart thundering in her chest. The words she had shouted—I won't let you take me—had barely been a whisper in the dark; a defiant cry in the face of overwhelming power. And yet, for the briefest of moments, something had stirred within her. A flicker of resistance, of something more than fear—something that defied the suffocating grip of the Hollow. The shadows had faltered for an instant, and the silence that followed had been almost deafening.

But now, the weight of the Hollow's presence seemed to return with renewed force. The air was thick with a strange, oppressive energy, as though the cavern itself was alive and breathing with malice. The walls seemed to pulse with the beat of something dark, ancient, and restless. And in the center of it all, Theo stood as an embodiment of everything the Hollow wanted her to become.

Eleanor tried to push the fear aside. She had to think. She had to find a way out—something, anything. The walls were closing in again. The shadows were thickening, and they were crawling toward her, as if they had a will of their own. But she couldn't let them win. She couldn't let Theo win.

Her eyes flickered to the stone altar at the center of the cavern. The carvings on its surface had shifted again, swirling in intricate patterns that were both beautiful and horrifying. They seemed to dance in the dim light, beckoning her, urging her to come closer. She could feel its pull, deep and insistent, like the force of gravity itself. But she resisted.

"What do you want from me?" Eleanor spat, her voice trembling with the weight of her fear and anger. She tried to sound confident, though she wasn't sure if the words were even meant for Theo or the Hollow. The cavern seemed to absorb her words, swallowing them whole.

Theo didn't answer. He only watched her, his face obscured by the shadows, though she could feel the weight of his gaze. His eyes were black, empty, a void that seemed to consume all light, all hope. There was no recognition in them—no trace of the Theo she had once known. Only the Hollow. Only the darkness.

"I never wanted this," she whispered, though she wasn't sure who she was speaking to anymore. Her mind raced, memories of their time together flashing before her eyes in rapid succession. They had been happy once, hadn't they? But something had changed. The moment they had stepped into this place, everything had shifted. Theo had changed. The Hollow had changed him, swallowed him whole, and now it was trying to do the same to her.

But she wasn't ready to let go. Not yet.

The shadows began to move again, crawling across the stone like living things. They swirled around her feet, tugging at her legs, pulling her down, down into the earth. The ground beneath her trembled, the cavern groaning as if it were alive and hungry, eager to devour her.

Eleanor stumbled backward, her heart racing. She looked around desperately for a way out, but the walls were too close, the passageways too narrow, and all she could see were the shifting shadows, closing in on her like a wave of darkness. The temperature dropped even further, the chill sinking deep into her bones, as though the very air had turned to ice.

"Choose."

The word came again, soft and insistent, like a whisper in the wind. It seemed to echo from all directions, surrounding her, pressing into her mind, into her soul. It was the same voice—the voice of the Hollow—and it was growing louder, more demanding with each passing moment. She clenched her fists, trying to block it out, but the words kept coming, relentless.

Choose or be consumed.

A flicker of something cold and sharp coursed through her chest, something dark that threatened to drown her in its weight. Was this it? Was this the moment? Was this where the Hollow would claim her, twist her into something unrecognizable, just as it had with Theo?

No.

Eleanor shook her head, desperate to hold on to herself, to hold on to the truth she had buried deep inside her. The Hollow was powerful, yes, but she wasn't as weak as it thought she was. She wasn't as weak as Theo had become. She still had something within her—the strength, the will to fight.

She could feel it, a flicker of fire buried deep in her chest, something that refused to be snuffed out. It was small, but it was there, and it was enough.

You've already made your choice.

The voice in her mind came again, almost mocking her now. The shadows hissed as they tightened around her, their coldness creeping further up her legs, curling around her waist, pulling her down. She struggled, her breath coming faster now, the weight of the darkness pressing in on her like an unrelenting force. Her hands trembled as she reached out to grasp the stone altar, as if it might offer some shred of salvation.

It's too late, the voice whispered, its words like poison, seeping into her thoughts. You are mine now.

For a moment, she felt a shudder of panic crawl up her spine. The voice was right. She had stepped into this place willingly. She had followed Theo. She had made her choice. There was no turning back.

But then, amidst the suffocating terror, something shifted. Eleanor's gaze snapped to the altar, to the swirling runes etched into its surface. They pulsed with an eerie light, flickering as though they were alive, as though they were responding to her. Her fingers brushed the cold stone, and a shock of energy jolted through her body. The force was so intense that she nearly cried out, but she kept her grip tight, refusing to let go.

For the first time since she had stepped into the Hollow, she felt something other than fear.

She felt power.

It wasn't the Hollow's power. It wasn't Theo's power. It was her own.

The shadows recoiled, as if startled by the surge of energy. They shrank back, momentarily dissipating, and Eleanor took a deep, shuddering breath, feeling the weight lift from her chest. The cavern seemed to pause, as if everything was waiting. Even the air felt still, suspended in time.

The voice came again, this time louder, almost furious.

No.

Eleanor's grip on the altar tightened. She could feel the pulse of the stone beneath her fingertips, the way it seemed to vibrate with energy. She could feel the magic of the Hollow—the power that had consumed Theo, that had twisted him into something unrecognizable—but now, for the first time, she could feel something else. She could feel herself.

And she would not let this place break her.

"No," she said aloud, the word feeling stronger now, more certain. "I will not be a part of you."

The ground trembled beneath her feet again, more violently this time. The shadows writhed and coiled like serpents, and the air crackled with the force of their fury. The walls of the cavern seemed to bend, shifting as if the space itself were warping under the weight of her resistance.

But Eleanor didn't waver. She held on, her mind focused, her will ironclad. The Hollow could take Theo, it could take this place, but it would not take her.

With a sudden surge of energy, she pushed against the altar, feeling the force of the stone respond to her. The runes on its surface flared, glowing brighter than ever, the light searing through the cavern, banishing the shadows that had once seemed all-encompassing. The cavern shuddered, and Eleanor felt the pressure on her chest lift as if the very air had been freed.

But even as the shadows receded, she could hear the whispers—faint, distant, but still present. They were not gone. Not yet. The Hollow was still there, lurking in the dark corners of her mind, waiting for her to falter.

But she would not falter.

Eleanor stepped back from the altar, her heart pounding in her chest, her body trembling from the exertion. Theo's eyes followed her every movement, his expression blank, empty—nothing but a shell.

"Choose," he whispered, his voice hollow, as if the words were not truly his own.

But Eleanor shook her head. "I choose myself."

And with that, she turned, walking toward the shadows, toward the only path she could see. The cavern would not claim her. Not today. Not ever.

11

Beneath the Surface

Eleanor's feet crunched against the rocky floor, each step echoing through the cavern, a soft, hollow sound that seemed to reverberate endlessly in the thick, oppressive silence. Her breath came in shallow gasps, the weight of her defiance still heavy in her chest, though the immediate pressure of the Hollow's grasp had eased—just slightly. She could still feel its presence, lurking in the dark corners of her mind, like an ever-present shadow.

The cold still gnawed at her skin, but now there was something else—a flicker of warmth, a tiny ember that burned fiercely in the pit of her stomach. It was fragile, like the first rays of sunlight breaking through the cracks in a stormy sky, but it was enough. Enough to keep her going. Enough to push her forward.

She wasn't free yet. Not by a long shot.

Her eyes flickered to the shadows around her, watching them

move, twist, and ripple with an unnatural energy. The Hollow was alive—alive in a way she hadn't yet understood, a living, breathing entity that thrived in the darkness. The air was thick with its malevolent presence, and each breath felt as though she were inhaling the very essence of the thing that had brought her to this place.

Theo's words—choose—still echoed in her mind, though the voice had quieted. But she couldn't stop thinking about them. Choose. What did it mean? Was it truly as simple as the Hollow said? Was her fate sealed by the mere act of stepping into this cavern? Or had she truly made a choice? And if she had, was it the right one?

Her steps slowed as she approached the mouth of a narrow passageway in the far corner of the cavern. The walls of the passage were slick with moisture, and the air had a musty, stagnant scent. She hesitated, feeling a growing unease settle in her chest. The shadows seemed to press in on her from all sides, their presence heavy and almost tangible.

She closed her eyes for a moment, taking a deep breath, gathering herself. She had to move forward. The Hollow couldn't have her. Not yet. Not if she could help it.

The narrow passage led deeper into the cavern, winding through tight, jagged turns, the walls pressing closer with every step she took. The air grew colder still, and she could feel the chill seeping into her bones, numbing her fingers and toes.

But still, she pressed on.

The sound of dripping water echoed through the passage, the steady rhythm filling the space, making it seem alive, as if the cavern itself was breathing. She reached out a hand to steady herself against the slick stone, her fingertips brushing against something strange—something slick and almost... organic. A shiver ran down her spine. It was as if the walls were alive, pulsing beneath her touch, soft and fleshy, a far cry from the solid stone she had expected.

With a sudden jolt of panic, she pulled her hand back, her heart racing. The flickering light from the torches she carried cast long, erratic shadows against the walls, but there was something else—something moving in the darkness. She froze, listening. The air felt charged now, electric, and her pulse quickened.

A sound, faint at first, echoed from deeper within the passage— low, guttural, almost like a growl. Her breath caught in her throat. She had never heard anything like it, and yet, somehow, it felt familiar. She wasn't alone. Something was in the shadows.

With a hesitant step, she moved forward again, her pulse pounding in her ears, the light from her torch trembling in her grip. Her eyes darted to every corner, every shadow, but the passage was narrow, and the darkness beyond her feeble light was impenetrable.

Another growl. Closer this time.

Her heart skipped in her chest. It was getting louder. The

sound of something breathing—something ancient and hungry. She tried to suppress the panic rising in her throat, but it was difficult. Every instinct told her to turn back, to flee from whatever lurked ahead, but she couldn't. Not now.

Not when she had come so far.

Her feet moved on their own, carrying her deeper into the passage, the walls growing closer together, the air growing colder still. She was nearing something—she could feel it, a presence at the edge of her consciousness. And the growls? They weren't growls at all. They were whispers.

Soft, taunting whispers, like fingers brushing against the back of her mind.

Come closer.

She froze. The voice—deep, guttural, but almost familiar—had come from the very walls. Her throat tightened, and she forced herself to take another step forward. The passage ahead opened up into a larger space, and as she stepped into the new chamber, the air shifted, growing heavier, as if the very atmosphere had changed.

The walls of the chamber were covered in strange markings, symbols etched into the stone, worn by centuries of erosion, yet still vibrant with an energy she couldn't place. The markings seemed to pulse with an unnatural life, shifting in the dim light like they were alive. She stepped forward cautiously, eyes wide, searching for the source of the strange energy she felt in the air.

Suddenly, the ground beneath her feet trembled, and the markings on the walls began to glow with an eerie, unnatural light. Eleanor stumbled backward, her breath catching in her throat as she struggled to maintain her balance. The whispering grew louder, the voices growing frantic, overlapping with each other, swirling around her like a windstorm.

She looked up and gasped.

In the center of the chamber, a stone pedestal rose from the ground, surrounded by the faint, flickering light of the symbols. Atop it, there was something. Something ancient and powerful. It was difficult to see clearly from where she stood, but it looked like a stone basin of sorts, its surface slick with an oily substance, shimmering in the dim light.

The growls—or rather, the whispers—came again. But now they weren't just in the air. They were in her mind.

Come closer, Eleanor.

Her heart skipped a beat as the realization hit her. This wasn't just a place. This wasn't just the Hollow. This was the very source—the heart of the Hollow. The power. The thing that had lured her here. The thing that had ensnared Theo. The thing that had been feeding off of her fear, her doubt, her uncertainty.

The stone basin seemed to beckon her, calling to her with an almost irresistible force. She could feel it now, the pulse of power emanating from it, pulling her in, wrapping around her, twisting her thoughts, her very being.

It was the same pull she had felt from the moment she set foot in the cavern—the pull of the Hollow. But this? This was different. This was real.

Without thinking, her feet carried her forward, and before she knew it, she was standing in front of the pedestal. The whispers were deafening now, filling her head, racing through her thoughts, drowning out everything else. She could feel the pull of the basin in her very bones, in the core of her being. She was close to something—close to understanding.

But a voice, her own voice, screamed inside her head, telling her to stop. To turn back.

And yet, her hand reached out.

Her fingers brushed the surface of the stone basin, and the world around her seemed to shudder. The whispers grew louder, more insistent, and the symbols on the walls blazed to life, their light searing into her eyes. The cold in the air intensified, and for a moment, she felt as though she were suffocating.

She pulled her hand back, gasping for air.

The whispers fell silent.

For a long moment, there was nothing but stillness. But in that silence, Eleanor could hear the truth. She could feel it deep within her, more clearly than ever before. The Hollow was not just a place—it was a force. A living entity that fed on fear, on doubt, on everything that made people weak. But she wasn't weak anymore.

She couldn't be.

And she wouldn't be.

Slowly, she stepped back, her breath steadying. The Hollow might have taken Theo, it might have tried to take her, but it would not win. Not here. Not now. Not if she could help it.

But as she turned to leave, a voice, deep and terrible, rumbled in her mind:

You cannot escape.

And though Eleanor's heart skipped a beat, her resolve only hardened. She had come too far.

12

The Weight of the Dark

The narrow tunnel behind Eleanor seemed to close in on her as she moved further into the labyrinth of the Hollow. Every step echoed, reverberating through the silence that pressed against her from all sides, a thick, suffocating weight that settled deep in her chest. Her heartbeat quickened, the sound of it drumming in her ears, drowning out all other noise. But still, the whispers from the walls—the voices that had taunted her and tempted her—lingered, their words growing fainter, but still present, like the remnants of a dream half-forgotten.

She couldn't shake the sensation that the cavern was watching her, the walls themselves alive, shifting with every passing moment. The sense of being stalked, of being hunted, hadn't abated. It was as though the Hollow was alive, a breathing, pulsating organism that lived off her fear, off her uncertainty. Every twist, every turn in the tunnel seemed to deepen the unsettling sense that the passageways were closing in around her.

Eleanor swallowed hard, trying to steady her breathing, trying to push the terror that clawed at her throat aside. She had faced worse before. She had come this far, hadn't she? She wasn't going to let fear take her now.

But something about the silence was different. It wasn't just the absence of sound—it was the absence of movement. The Hollow was still there, lurking beneath the surface of everything, but it wasn't pushing her anymore. It was waiting. Waiting for her to make the next move.

The dim light from her torch flickered, casting erratic shadows along the walls, and the air grew colder, the chill sinking deeper into her bones. She pulled her cloak tighter around her shoulders, trying to ward off the cold, but it was no use. The temperature in the cavern seemed to drop with each step, and it wasn't just the physical cold she felt. It was as though the very atmosphere itself had turned inhospitable, suffocating.

Then, she heard it.

A sound, faint at first, but unmistakable. A soft, scraping noise, like something—someone—moving in the darkness behind her.

Her heart skipped a beat. She froze, her entire body going rigid as she strained to listen. The noise was faint, too quiet to be certain, but it was there. It was like the sound of boots on stone—deliberate, slow, purposeful.

Eleanor's pulse quickened. She wanted to look behind her,

to confirm whether it was real or just the product of her imagination, but she didn't. Every instinct screamed at her not to turn around, to keep moving forward, to keep pushing through the dark.

But as she moved further, the sound followed, steady and unyielding. Whoever—or whatever—was out there, it was tracking her.

She took a deep breath, forcing herself to move. She had to find a way out, but it was impossible to know which direction to take. The labyrinth of stone and shadow seemed endless, each turn more disorienting than the last. It felt as though the Hollow itself was alive, shifting the paths, twisting them, as though it wanted her to get lost.

Another scrape of movement, this time closer, sharper. Eleanor's breath caught in her throat, and she broke into a run, her footsteps echoing against the cold stone floor. Her torch light flickered wildly, casting distorted shapes on the walls as she sprinted forward, her heart thundering in her chest. The sound of pursuit was growing louder now—closer—and her mind raced as she tried to figure out who or what could be chasing her. Was it Theo? Had the Hollow somehow twisted him into something else, something monstrous?

She couldn't afford to look back. She couldn't afford to hesitate. But the sound grew, and the shadows seemed to stretch and fold in on her from all sides. She turned another corner, her legs burning with the effort, but the air seemed to press tighter around her, closing in like a vice.

Suddenly, the path before her opened up into a wide cavern, much larger than the twisting passageways she had navigated. She stumbled into the center, her breath coming in ragged gasps, the torch in her hand shaking so violently that the flame sputtered and nearly died. But she didn't stop. The shadows still pursued her, snapping at her heels like an unseen predator.

The cavern was vast, the ceiling disappearing into darkness, and at the far end of the room, Eleanor could just make out the faint outline of something standing still—a figure, unmoving, but waiting.

A voice, deep and guttural, rippled through the air, a low growl that was unmistakably human, but twisted and broken. Eleanor...

Her heart skipped in her chest, and she froze. The voice was unmistakable. It was Theo. But the Theo who had spoken was not the one she knew. The words were distorted, thick with a hunger that made her skin crawl.

The figure at the far end of the cavern shifted slightly, and Eleanor's heart pounded in her ears as she squinted to make sense of it. The air felt dense in the chamber, heavy with an electric charge, as though the very space were charged with something dark, something ancient.

She hesitated, fear tightening its grip on her chest, but the truth was undeniable. The Hollow had done this. It had twisted Theo's very soul. It had transformed him, like a puppeteer manipulating a marionette, and now it was sending him after her.

"Theo?" Eleanor's voice trembled despite her best efforts. "Please... please, stop."

The figure took a step forward, and she could make out the jagged silhouette of him in the dim light. He was still Theo—still the man she had once loved, but there was something wrong about him. His face was gaunt, hollowed out, and his eyes were dark pools of emptiness, endless voids that seemed to suck the light from the room. His clothes hung from him like tattered rags, his form impossibly thin, his movements jerky and unnatural.

He looked at her, but it wasn't the look of someone she knew. It wasn't love or recognition. It was something far darker, more primal.

"Come closer, Eleanor," his voice rasped, barely a whisper, but it carried across the cavern with frightening clarity. "The Hollow has been waiting for you. It's waiting for us."

Eleanor took a step back, her breath catching in her throat. The fear threatened to overtake her, but she couldn't let it. Not now. Not when she was so close.

"You're not Theo," she whispered, shaking her head, though her voice was barely audible over the sound of her own pulse hammering in her ears. "You're not him."

He tilted his head to the side, as though confused by her words.

His lips parted, and Eleanor could see the shadows moving beneath his skin, the flickers of dark energy that seemed to pulse with life.

"I am Theo," he said, and this time, there was a crack in his voice, a tremor of something that might have been sorrow—or regret—beneath the darkness. "But I'm not the only one."

The shadows behind him seemed to ripple, and suddenly, the cavern was alive with movement. Figures began to emerge from the dark, shapes that were more than human, twisted versions of men and women, their faces obscured, their eyes black voids. They moved with a strange, jerky motion, as though they were puppets whose strings had been pulled too tightly.

Eleanor's breath caught in her throat. They were shadows of the people who had come before her—twisted, tortured, and broken by the Hollow. They had all come here, looking for answers, looking for escape, and now they were just empty shells, walking extensions of the darkness that had consumed them.

Theo's voice came again, softer now, almost a plea. "Join us, Eleanor. You can still be one of us. You can still be free."

Eleanor's legs trembled, but she forced herself to stand firm, pushing the terror down, ignoring the sharp pulse of fear that rattled her bones. She had to resist. She had to fight.

"I won't be like you," she said, her voice gaining strength. "I won't let the Hollow take me."

Theo's eyes narrowed, the darkness in them swirling as if stirred by her words.

"It's not your choice anymore," he whispered. "It was never your choice."

The cavern trembled beneath her feet. The walls groaned as if the Hollow itself were responding to his words, its power gathering like a storm. The figures surrounding her moved closer, their feet dragging across the stone floor, their presence pressing in on her like the weight of the world.

But Eleanor didn't move. She didn't give in.

She was not like them. Not yet.

13

The Waking Nightmare

Eleanor's body felt heavy, as though the air around her had thickened into something solid, something oppressive. The figures surrounding her continued moving closer, their hollow eyes watching her with a detached, eerie stillness, as if they were waiting for something—waiting for her to break, to falter. The cold that had seeped into her skin now seemed to penetrate deeper, twisting inside her very bones, gnawing away at her strength.

She swallowed hard, her throat dry. The shadows pressed in on all sides, their figures indistinct but growing in number, their movements unnerving—like puppets controlled by a dark, invisible hand. She could feel the air growing denser, heavier, as if the cavern itself were holding its breath, anticipating something.

And then there was Theo.

He was no longer moving, just standing at the far edge of the cavern, his eyes fixed on her, his face an unreadable mask. The emptiness in his gaze made her heart ache, but she refused to let it consume her. He wasn't Theo anymore—not truly. The Hollow had changed him. And that was the truth she couldn't let herself forget.

"You're not him," she whispered under her breath, repeating it like a mantra, trying to convince herself more than anyone else.

But the figures continued to gather, their presence suffocating, the space around her shrinking as the air grew colder. The whispers—those low, guttural voices that had once seemed so distant—now flooded her mind, swirling through her thoughts like a tide that wouldn't recede. She could hear their words, though they made no sense, just fragments of broken phrases, twisted, warped by the same force that had claimed Theo.

Come closer. Join us. You cannot fight us.

Her skin prickled as if the cavern itself were alive, breathing, pulsing with dark energy. The shadows seemed to shift, their forms flickering like half-remembered nightmares, and Eleanor felt an overwhelming sense of dread close in, suffocating her, suffusing the very air around her. The Hollow had found a way to dig into her mind, its tendrils wrapping around her thoughts, pulling at her resolve.

But Eleanor's breath was steady. Her grip on the torch in her hand tightened as she forced herself to remain calm, even though every instinct in her body screamed at her to run—to escape the suffocating dark.

Theo's voice broke through the silence once more, this time softer, tinged with something that almost felt like desperation. "Please, Eleanor... don't you see? You don't have to fight. We can be together again. I can take you away from this place. The Hollow will protect us. It will protect you."

Her heart twisted, her mind spinning with the possibility of Theo returning to her, of the love they had once shared before the Hollow had claimed him. But that fleeting hope was a lie, a cruel trick.

"No." Her voice was firm now, the weight of the word grounding her. "I won't let you drag me down with you. You're not the Theo I knew. I won't let the Hollow win."

The words hung in the air like a challenge. The cavern seemed to breathe with her, the walls closing in just slightly, the whispers intensifying. She could feel them—the shadows, the figures, the presence of the Hollow itself—closing in. They were ready to swallow her whole. But she couldn't give in. Not when she was this close to understanding.

Not when she was this close to freedom.

Suddenly, without warning, Theo moved. His body jerked, the motion unnatural, like a broken puppet being forced to walk. The others followed suit, their limbs twitching, dragging themselves forward with jerky, unsettling movements. The cavern was alive with a horrible, scraping sound, the echo of their steps reverberating through the stone.

And then, just as quickly, they stopped.

The silence in the cavern was absolute. For a moment, it seemed as though the entire world had paused. The shadows were still. The whispers had ceased.

It was as if the cavern had stopped breathing.

Eleanor's pulse raced, her hand trembling as she gripped the torch tighter, its light flickering in the heavy air. She could feel it—the tension in the air, the weight of the moment before something inevitable.

Then the voice came again. This time, it wasn't Theo's. It was deeper, more resonant, as if it came from the very heart of the Hollow itself.

"You are a fool, Eleanor."

The words rippled through the air like a thunderclap, shaking her to the core. The walls trembled in response, the ground beneath her feet shifting like a living thing. She staggered, unsteady, but caught herself. Her heart beat faster, her mind racing, as she tried to comprehend the magnitude of the voice, the power it wielded.

"You think you can escape. You think you can defeat me. But you're wrong." The voice grew louder, filling every corner of the cavern. "You are mine now. Just like the others."

The figures surrounding her began to move again, their pace slow, deliberate. Their faces were obscured in shadow, but she could feel their gaze on her, a pressure that made her skin crawl. The air had grown colder, biting at her skin, but it wasn't just the temperature. It was the weight of their presence, their intentions. The Hollow had claimed them, just as it had claimed Theo. And now it was reaching for her.

"You're wrong," she said, her voice shaking but defiant. She took a step back, the torch raised in front of her like a shield. The light flickered wildly, but she forced herself to hold it steady. "I'm not like them. I won't be like them."

The voice laughed. A low, terrible sound that echoed off the walls and reverberated through her bones. "You think you have a choice?" it asked, the question dripping with mockery. "There is no escape, Eleanor. The Hollow feeds on your fear, on your pain, and you have given it everything. You're already mine. And once you're mine, there's no going back."

Her heart pounded in her chest as the cavern seemed to close in around her. The figures were nearly upon her now, their steps purposeful, as if they had been waiting for her to crumble under the weight of their words.

But Eleanor wouldn't. She couldn't.

She swallowed hard, forcing herself to take another step back, but the cavern seemed to stretch farther, each step she took causing the shadows to grow longer, the figures to draw closer. It was as though the Hollow itself were warping the space around her, pushing her into a corner from which there was no escape.

But then, just as she felt the walls closing in—just as her breath quickened and her vision blurred—the ground beneath her feet gave way.

With a startled cry, Eleanor fell, tumbling into the darkness, the torch falling from her grasp, its light disappearing into the abyss. Her body collided with something hard, and she gasped, pain shooting up her spine. For a moment, everything was still, silent. The cold, suffocating air pressed in from all sides, and she couldn't tell if she had fallen into some new chamber, or if she had simply been swallowed whole.

Her hands scraped against the rough stone as she tried to push herself up, the darkness enveloping her, thick and inescapable. She tried to focus, to push back the fear that was threatening to overtake her, but she could feel it—like a presence, like a heavy weight pressing down on her chest.

And then, through the dark, through the cold, came a voice.

"You're in my domain now."

Eleanor's breath caught in her throat. The words were familiar—more familiar than she wanted to admit. The Hollow had taken her here, deeper than she had ever gone before, into the very heart of its power.

She was alone. She was lost.

But she wasn't defeated. Not yet.

Not as long as she still had breath in her body.

14

The Breaking Point

The darkness pressed in on Eleanor, suffocating, unyielding, as if the cavern itself had opened its mouth to swallow her whole. Her heart pounded in her chest, each beat a thunderous drum in the silence that surrounded her. The torch she had dropped was nowhere to be seen, its flame extinguished the moment it had left her grasp. The cold was unbearable, settling deep into her bones, its icy tendrils crawling beneath her skin.

She had fallen deeper than she had ever anticipated. The Hollow had a way of distorting reality, twisting the space around her, making her feel as though she were caught in some terrible dream—one that she couldn't wake from.

Eleanor's breath came in ragged gasps as she tried to push herself to her feet. The stone beneath her was jagged, sharp, and unyielding. She winced as she placed one hand on the floor, feeling the rough texture scrape against her skin. The chill of the stone seeped into her bones, yet she refused to let it break her. She wouldn't let the Hollow win.

It had taken Theo. It had taken everyone who had ever come close to her. She could still hear his voice echoing in the recesses of her mind, twisted and broken, pleading for her to join him. It had been the voice of a man she had once loved. A man who had been consumed, devoured by the darkness that now surrounded her.

But she wasn't going to let it take her, too.

She forced herself to rise, her body trembling from the effort, her legs unsteady as she pushed off the ground. The cold seemed to swallow her breath, but she breathed through it, focusing on the task at hand. She needed to get out. She needed to find a way to stop whatever was happening here before it consumed her completely.

The air was thick with a strange, unsettling energy. She could feel it in the walls, in the ground beneath her feet. The Hollow was close—closer than it had ever been. It was everywhere, pressing in on her, alive in a way that made her skin crawl. She could feel the shadows shifting in the corners of her mind, pulling at her thoughts, threatening to swallow her consciousness.

With every step she took, the darkness seemed to grow thicker, more oppressive. The shadows twisted and writhed, whispering in voices that she couldn't quite understand. She tried to ignore them, tried to focus on the task at hand. But the Hollow was relentless. Its presence was all-encompassing.

Her legs felt as though they were made of lead as she stumbled forward, each step heavier than the last. It was as if the very ground was working against her, pulling her down, refusing to let her escape. She could feel the walls closing in, the air growing colder, the pressure building around her. The Hollow was closing in.

The silence was maddening. She could hear nothing but her own breath, the pounding of her heart in her ears. But then, a sound pierced the silence—faint at first, but unmistakable.

A low, guttural growl.

Eleanor froze, her blood running cold. She wasn't alone.

The growl came again, louder this time, more insistent. It was the sound of something—someone—moving through the darkness toward her. The air seemed to vibrate with the intensity of it, like a predator closing in on its prey.

Her body went stiff, panic rising like a tidal wave in her chest. She wanted to turn and run, to flee into the dark corners of the cavern where she could hide, where she could escape the inevitable confrontation. But there was nowhere to run. She had no idea where she was, no idea which way to go. The Hollow had already twisted the world around her into a nightmare, and every path she had taken had only led her deeper into its grip.

The growl was closer now, just beyond her reach. She could feel it—a presence, a force in the darkness. It was coming for her.

Eleanor's breath hitched in her throat as she instinctively took a step back, her heart racing in her chest. The shadows seemed to shift again, bending and swirling around her like a living thing. She couldn't see anything—couldn't hear anything except the oppressive silence and the sound of her own pulse hammering in her ears.

And then, out of the darkness, a figure stepped forward.

Theo.

But it wasn't the Theo she remembered.

His form was warped, twisted, as if the Hollow had molded him into something else entirely. His face was gaunt, hollowed out, the skin stretched tight over his bones. His eyes—once warm, once full of life—were now deep pools of nothingness, black and empty, as if the light had been drained from them entirely. His mouth hung slightly open, but no words came out—only a low, guttural moan that sent chills down Eleanor's spine.

Eleanor's breath caught in her throat.

"No," she whispered, her voice trembling, but defiant. "No, you're not him. You're not Theo."

But the figure that stood before her didn't move. It didn't speak. It just stood there, watching her with those empty, soulless eyes.

The growl came again, louder now, as if the very walls of the cavern were trembling in response. The shadows around them shifted, drawing in closer, feeding on the fear that radiated from her. Eleanor's chest tightened, and for a moment, she couldn't breathe.

The Hollow was here. It had found her. And it had brought Theo with it.

Her pulse thudded in her ears, the noise deafening in the stillness. She had to move—had to do something. She could feel the weight of the darkness pressing down on her, and if she didn't act now, it would consume her entirely.

Taking a deep breath, Eleanor forced herself to step forward.

"I won't let you take me," she said, her voice growing stronger, more resolute. She gritted her teeth, trying to push back the wave of fear that was threatening to drown her. "You can't have me."

The figure of Theo jerked, its head tilting at an unnatural angle, as though considering her words. For a split second, there was a flicker—just a flicker—of recognition in his eyes. Something human. Something real.

But it was gone in an instant, replaced by the hollow emptiness that had consumed him. The growl returned, deeper this time, vibrating the very walls around them. And the figure—Theo—lunged.

Eleanor didn't have time to think. She barely had time to react.

She dodged, rolling to the side as the figure crashed into the ground where she had been standing just a moment before. The force of the impact shook the cavern, sending dust and debris flying through the air. The walls groaned, as if the very earth was trembling in response.

Eleanor scrambled to her feet, her heart racing. The shadows closed in, swirling around her, the growls rising from all sides. The figure of Theo was rising again, its body jerking and twitching as though it were being controlled by some unseen force.

She had no time. She had no time to think.

The Hollow had her cornered.

But something inside her—something deep within her—flared to life. A spark of defiance, of strength, ignited within her chest. She couldn't give up. Not now. Not when she was so close.

"Leave me alone!" she screamed, her voice a raw, primal shout that echoed through the cavern.

The shadows recoiled for a moment, as if taken aback by her words. For a brief second, the growling stopped. The figure of Theo hesitated.

And in that moment, Eleanor grabbed the closest thing she could find—a jagged rock, sharp and heavy. She swung it at the figure with all her strength, the impact making a sickening crack as the stone collided with its skull.

Theo staggered backward, his body jerking with the force of the blow. The shadows faltered, retreating just a step.

For a fleeting moment, Eleanor thought she might have a chance. But the voice of the Hollow cut through the stillness once again, low and mocking.

"You think a mere rock will stop me?"

The ground trembled beneath her feet. The figure of Theo lurched forward again, more vicious this time. The shadows surged around her, the growling rising to a deafening roar.

And Eleanor realized, in that terrifying moment, that she was at the breaking point. There was no escaping this. There was no way out.

Her body shook, but her will was unbroken. Not yet.

Not as long as she still had breath in her body.

15

The Fractured Reflection

Eleanor's heart hammered in her chest, a frantic rhythm that drowned out everything around her. The shadows closed in, twisting and writhing like dark snakes, creeping toward her with a malevolent purpose. Her breath came in ragged gasps, her body trembling as she clutched the jagged rock in her hand, the only weapon she had against the oncoming tide of terror.

The figure of Theo, now barely recognizable, staggered forward, its limbs jerking unnaturally as if each movement were forced, unnatural. His hollow eyes—empty, black voids—stared through her, and the weight of that gaze felt like a physical blow. The growling noise was almost deafening now, reverberating through the very air, vibrating in her chest, sending waves of nausea spiraling through her.

For a moment, she thought she saw something flicker in those empty eyes—a glimmer of recognition, perhaps, or something more human, something that reached out from the depths of the Hollow's grasp. But then it was gone, swallowed whole by the blackness. He was lost.

And she was alone.

The ground trembled beneath her feet, a low, guttural rumble that seemed to rise from the very depths of the earth. The shadows surrounding her seemed to pulse, each flicker of darkness twisting into a new form, a new terror. Eleanor's chest tightened, her pulse quickening as the realization hit her: she was trapped. There was no way out of this.

The cavern stretched on forever, an endless expanse of stone and shadow. No escape. No way back to the surface. Just the oppressive, suffocating weight of the Hollow's influence, closing in from all sides.

The figure of Theo lunged at her again, its movements jerky, unpredictable. Eleanor sidestepped, her feet sliding against the slick stone as she dodged. But the darkness had its hold on her, a grip that tightened with each passing second. The growling, that horrifying noise, reverberated in her bones, making it impossible to think. The shadows themselves were closing in, surrounding her, suffocating her. The cold air grew heavier, thicker. The scent of damp stone and decay filled her nostrils, mingling with the fear that stank like rot in her throat.

She couldn't fight it anymore. The Hollow had won. Theo was lost to it, and there was nothing left of him. Nothing but this twisted, broken version of the man she had once loved. He was gone, and the Hollow had claimed him.

Eleanor's mind reeled, her thoughts spiraling out of control. She couldn't keep running. She couldn't keep fighting. She couldn't keep pretending that there was hope.

And then, just as all of that suffocating despair threatened to swallow her whole, she heard it.

A voice.

Faint. So faint that she wasn't sure it was real at first. But it was there, in the space between the growls, the chaos, the endless noise.

"Eleanor..."

Her name.

The voice was familiar, but it didn't belong to Theo. It was soft, desperate, a whisper carried on the wind. She whipped around, her eyes wide with panic, searching the dark. Her breath caught in her throat, and for a moment, her heart stopped.

A figure. Standing at the edge of the cavern, just beyond the reach of the shadows. The flicker of a light—was it a torch? A lantern? It glowed dimly, but it was enough to cut through the oppressive darkness that surrounded her.

"Eleanor..." the voice repeated.

It was her name, but it wasn't Theo. It was a voice she hadn't heard in so long—one she thought had been lost to the darkness, lost to time.

"Ugochi?" she whispered, the name barely leaving her lips. She couldn't believe it. She shouldn't believe it. But the pull of that voice—the familiarity, the hope it brought—was enough to break through the crushing weight of fear that had paralyzed her.

The figure moved forward, emerging from the shadows, the light flickering weakly in their hand. It was a woman—tall, strong, with braided hair pulled back into a tight bun. Ugochi. Eleanor's breath caught in her throat as she took a cautious step forward.

But as Ugochi's face came into view, Eleanor's heart sank.

It wasn't Ugochi. Not really.

The woman's eyes were dark, but not with the warmth and kindness that Eleanor remembered. They were empty, just like Theo's. Hollow. A mirror of the same thing that had claimed everyone she loved.

Ugochi—if it even was her—smiled. But it was a twisted, sickening grin that sent a chill through Eleanor's spine. Her skin, once radiant, was now deathly pale. Her clothes were torn and stained with something that resembled blood. Her hands—clawed, jagged—reached toward Eleanor, and the air around them seemed to grow colder, darker.

"Ugochi..." Eleanor whispered, her voice trembling. "No... this isn't you. This isn't real."

The woman—Ugochi—laughed, a low, mocking sound that echoed through the cavern, reverberating off the walls like the crackling of a fire. The shadows seemed to grow with her laughter, the darkness twisting and shifting as if it were alive.

"You think you can escape it, Eleanor?" the woman said, her voice dripping with malice. "You think you can fight it? It's too late. You're already part of it. You've always been part of it."

The words were like poison, seeping into Eleanor's mind, twisting her thoughts, digging into her soul. She shook her head, trying to push the words away, but the more she fought, the more they seemed to take root.

The air felt thick now—impossible to breathe. She gasped for air, but it was as though the cavern had become a tomb, closing in around her. Ugochi's form seemed to flicker, like a mirage, the shadows around her warping and distorting, making it impossible to tell what was real and what was just a reflection of the Hollow's influence.

"No," Eleanor whispered again, but this time her voice faltered. She was starting to believe it. She was starting to believe the Hollow had already taken her. That there was no way out. No escape from the suffocating grip of darkness.

But then, through the fog of despair, another voice broke through. Faint. Faint, but unmistakable.

"Eleanor... you are stronger than this."

She froze, her heart stuttering in her chest. The voice was calm, steady. It was one she recognized, but hadn't heard in what felt like years.

Dapo.

Her mind raced, her breath catching in her throat. Dapo—how? How could he be here? He had been lost. He had been swallowed by the same darkness that had claimed Theo.

But his voice... it was real. It wasn't the hollow whisper of the Hollow. It wasn't the growl of the shadows. It was his. Strong. Unyielding.

"Fight," the voice urged. "Fight for what's left of you. Fight for him. Fight for Theo."

The words were like a lifeline thrown into the abyss. Her head spun, her heart battered in her chest, but the surge of hope was enough to stop the darkness from swallowing her whole. She wasn't alone. She couldn't be. Not if Dapo was still out there. Not if Theo's humanity—however small—was still there.

With a gasp, Eleanor pushed forward, shoving past the twisted reflection of Ugochi. The shadows recoiled, retreating slightly, but not enough. The growls, the murmurs of the Hollow, filled her ears, but they no longer held the same power over her.

"Dapo!" she cried, her voice shaking with the force of the words.

"Dapo! I'm coming!"

The shadows lunged again, the growling escalating to a roar. But Eleanor didn't stop. The reflection of Ugochi—if it could still be called that—reached out for her, but she swatted it away, the jagged stone still in her hand. The Hollow, the darkness, the voices—they no longer mattered.

She could feel the light—the real light—drawing closer. Dapo's voice was the beacon she needed.

And just as the darkness reached for her one final time, Eleanor threw herself into the light, determined to reach the surface, to break free.

The cavern trembled, as if it knew it was losing its hold on her.

16

The Edge of All Things

The world spun around Eleanor, a kaleidoscope of twisting shadows and blinding light. She could feel the air thickening, her breath coming in gasps as if she were drowning in it. Each step forward felt like wading through a sea of impossibility, and yet, somehow, she moved. The voice of Dapo, distant but real, urged her onward. But what lay ahead? Was this the way out, or was it yet another cruel illusion created by the Hollow?

Her heart raced, pumping a mixture of fear and adrenaline through her veins. Her fingers, wrapped tightly around the jagged rock, trembled in time with the beat of her pulse. The cavern walls around her twisted, their jagged faces distorting and shifting, as if trying to trap her once again. The ground beneath her feet seemed to slant at impossible angles, each step becoming more difficult than the last, as if the earth itself was trying to throw her off balance.

And the voices. They were back—soft at first, like whispers from the corner of her mind, but they quickly grew louder. They were everywhere now, filling her head with their incessant murmurs.

"You cannot escape."

"You are nothing."

"We are your only truth."

Eleanor's chest tightened, and her breath quickened as she pushed forward, her mind racing. She could almost feel the Hollow closing in around her, its oppressive weight pressing down from all sides. The shadows twisted in the corners of her vision, their tendrils reaching for her, pulling at her thoughts, threatening to suffocate her. But she couldn't let them. Not now.

She had come too far to turn back. She had seen the truth in Theo's eyes, and she had heard Dapo's voice. She had felt their presence—fragments of something real amidst the darkness. And she refused to believe that the Hollow could take that from her. She had a choice. She had to believe that she still had a choice.

"Dapo?" she whispered, her voice trembling, barely more than a breath. "Are you there?"

For a moment, there was silence. A deafening silence, thick with the weight of her question. Then, as if from the depths of the earth itself, she heard the faintest echo.

"I'm here."

It wasn't just a voice. It was a pulse, a heartbeat that resonated through her very soul. Dapo's presence filled the air, surrounding her, grounding her in a way she hadn't felt in what seemed like an eternity.

And then the ground shifted beneath her feet, the cavern itself groaning, its walls trembling as though the very fabric of the Hollow was beginning to crack. The whispers of the shadows grew louder, now more insistent, more desperate.

"You cannot fight us."

"You are ours, Eleanor. Forever."

The voice was no longer Dapo's. It was the Hollow's. The same malevolent force that had claimed Theo, Ugochi, and so many others. Eleanor's hands clenched tighter around the stone, her knuckles white as the weight of those words pressed down on her.

But she didn't stop. She couldn't stop.

The path ahead of her grew narrower, the walls pressing in, suffocating, like a tomb closing around her. But there was no turning back now. She could feel it—a pull, a force—guiding her toward something just beyond the reach of her vision. Something she couldn't quite grasp but knew she had to reach. It was a light, distant but undeniable, shining with an intensity that burned brighter than the darkest shadows.

With every step she took, the ground trembled harder. The air thickened. The whispering voices swirled around her, growing into a cacophony of conflicting emotions: rage, fear, sorrow, despair. It was all there, fighting for dominance in her mind. The Hollow wanted her to lose control, wanted her to be swallowed whole by the darkness.

But she was stronger than that.

Eleanor's steps faltered for only a moment. A shadow appeared ahead of her—a dark, indistinct figure that seemed to shift with the movement of the air itself. Her breath caught in her throat as she froze, the world narrowing to a single point of fear. But then, she saw it—the flicker of light behind the figure, brighter than ever, calling to her.

Without thinking, she surged forward, the jagged rock in her hand raised defensively. The figure in front of her jerked toward her, its form blurry, almost formless.

And then it spoke.

"Eleanor... you cannot outrun fate."

The voice was familiar—too familiar—and for a moment, Eleanor thought her heart would stop. It was Theo. His voice, once warm and full of love, now twisted into something dark, something menacing.

"Let me go, Theo," she said, her voice breaking with the weight of his name. She refused to let herself break. She refused to let the Hollow win.

"Why do you fight, Eleanor?" The figure took a step toward her, the shadows surrounding it like a cloak. "You cannot change what is. You cannot change me. You cannot save him."

The words stung, deep inside her chest, as though they were pulling at something fragile, something buried beneath layers of pain and memories. But she wouldn't let it. She couldn't let the Hollow destroy what was left of her.

"Because I still believe in him," she said, her voice gaining strength. "I still believe in the man you were. In the man I loved."

The figure faltered for a moment, its form flickering like a candle in the wind. A faint shadow of recognition passed through its eyes—if they could still be called eyes.

"You..." it whispered, and for a brief instant, Eleanor thought she saw Theo, truly saw him, standing before her, not the Hollow, not the thing that had taken him.

But then the shadows overtook him again, and the darkness returned.

"Do not let the past define you," the figure hissed. "You are nothing without me. Nothing without the Hollow."

The words hit her like a physical blow, and for a moment, Eleanor felt the crushing weight of them settle over her chest.

She could feel herself buckling under the force of them, the desire to give in tugging at her mind.

But then she remembered Dapo's voice. She remembered the warmth of the connection they had shared, the strength he had given her when she had thought she had nothing left. She remembered the fragments of Theo's humanity that still lingered, faint but undeniable.

She wasn't alone. Not anymore.

The light ahead of her flared brighter, and without thinking, Eleanor lunged forward, pushing the darkness aside with the strength of her will. The figure of Theo twisted in her vision, but she didn't stop. She couldn't stop.

And then, as if by sheer force of will, she broke through.

The world around her shattered.

The shadows recoiled, the oppressive weight of the Hollow lifting for a moment, as if the very fabric of reality was torn open. Eleanor's breath hitched in her chest, and her body trembled from the sudden release. For a split second, she thought she might be free.

But then, she saw it.

The edge of all things.

It was a rift, a crack in the very fabric of existence itself. Beyond it, there was nothing—just an endless expanse of darkness, stretching on into eternity. And yet, at the center of it all, was the faintest glimmer of light.

Eleanor stepped toward the edge, her heart racing, her body shaking. The light called to her, and she couldn't resist. The pull was too strong.

"Dapo," she whispered, her voice shaking with the weight of everything she had lost, everything she had fought for. "I'm coming."

But as she stepped closer to the rift, something shifted.

The ground trembled again, and the Hollow's voice rose, louder than ever, filling her head with its relentless whispers. It was too late, the voice said. She had already lost. The light was an illusion. There was no escape.

The rift stretched wider, its edges jagged and unstable. Eleanor's heart pounded as she stared into the abyss beyond it. The light—the hope—was just out of reach.

And then, with one final, desperate breath, she took the step that would either lead her to salvation or to the very heart of the Hollow itself.

The edge of all things was before her, and she had no choice but to fall.

17

The Hollow Within

Eleanor's heart raced as she stepped forward, the rift expanding before her like the jaws of some great beast, waiting to devour her whole. The ground beneath her feet seemed to shift, the very earth trembling as though it, too, felt the force of what was about to happen. The abyss beyond the rift stretched into infinity, a vast void that threatened to swallow her entire existence.

The light that had once been her beacon now flickered, growing weaker, as though even the hope it represented was slowly being suffocated by the relentless pull of the darkness. Her breath caught in her throat as the realization dawned on her— this was it. There was no turning back. No more running. No more hiding. She was at the edge, not just of the rift, but of everything she had fought for.

Her fingers tightened around the jagged stone she had held for so long, the only weapon she had against the consuming dark. The weight of it felt insignificant now. She could feel the coldness of the abyss seeping into her bones, its chill more real than anything she had ever known. The walls of the cavern had crumbled away, and all that was left was this—this endless expanse of nothingness. She was alone.

"Dapo…" she whispered, her voice barely more than a breath, as though speaking his name might make him appear at her side. But the only sound that returned was the relentless hum of the Hollow, that insidious noise that filled her skull, gnawing at the edges of her sanity. It was the same hum she had heard when Theo first succumbed to the darkness, the same noise that had followed her through the caves, the same sound that now threatened to pull her under.

The abyss before her seemed to pulse, its rhythm matching the frantic beat of her heart. The darkness was alive, a force beyond her comprehension, something ancient and vast, something that fed on despair, on hopelessness. It was the Hollow. It had always been the Hollow.

But she refused to give in.

Eleanor took another step forward, her feet trembling, her legs threatening to give way beneath her. She had seen too much. She had felt the weight of loss too many times to surrender to this. She had seen the remnants of her loved ones—Theo, Ugochi, Dapo—lost to the shadows, their very beings twisted and corrupted by the Hollow's influence. But in each of them, she had seen something more. She had seen fragments of the people they once were, hidden beneath the darkness, waiting to be found. And she believed that if she could just push through, if she could just reach the light, she could save them.

She could save herself.

The pull of the abyss was unbearable now, like invisible hands reaching for her, dragging at her very soul. Her breath became shallow, the weight of the darkness pressing in from all sides. She could feel the edges of her vision blur, the shadows closing in, threatening to overtake her. But even as the darkness clawed at her, she pressed on, one step at a time, her resolve hardening with each passing moment.

"Please," she whispered to the void, her voice barely audible over the crashing roar of the Hollow. "I'm not giving up. I won't give up."

As if in response, the shadows before her shifted. The swirling blackness seemed to pulse and writhe, and for a brief moment, Eleanor thought she saw something—someone—standing at the center of the rift. It was a figure, tall and shadowed, its features obscured by the darkness. But even from this distance, she could feel the pull of it, like a magnetic force drawing her toward it.

Her heart skipped a beat. Could it be? Was it Dapo? Was it Theo? Had they somehow returned from the clutches of the Hollow?

Eleanor didn't hesitate. She moved forward, her feet steady despite the swirling chaos that surrounded her. The figure in the rift was closer now, its form becoming more distinct, its presence stronger. As she drew nearer, she could see the outline of a face, pale and hollow, the eyes dark voids that seemed to look right through her.

"No," she whispered, her voice trembling with fear. "No, this isn't you."

The figure stepped forward, and as it did, the shadows seemed to part, revealing more of its form. The face of the figure was familiar, but it wasn't Dapo. It wasn't Theo. It was something else—something more terrifying. The figure's skin was ashen, its eyes dark pits of emptiness, and its smile was a twisted mockery of the ones she had once known. It was not a person. It was the Hollow, taking on the form of her loved ones, twisting their faces into something unrecognizable.

"Eleanor..." the voice rasped, the same voice she had heard echoing in her mind, the same voice that had once whispered her name with warmth and love. Now it was laced with malice, twisted beyond recognition. "I've been waiting for you."

The words sent a shiver down Eleanor's spine. She stopped in her tracks, the chill of fear settling over her like a cold blanket. Her eyes locked onto the figure, and for a moment, she couldn't look away. It wasn't Theo. It wasn't Dapo. It was the Hollow itself—manifested before her, showing her the worst version of everything she had lost.

"Why are you doing this?" she asked, her voice barely more than a whisper. She could feel the weight of the abyss closing in on her, but she refused to turn away. "What do you want from me?"

The figure stepped closer, the air around them growing colder with each passing second. "I want you," it said, its voice a cold, cruel mockery. "I want you to join us. To become one with the Hollow. To embrace what you truly are."

The words cut through her like a blade. She could feel the darkness inside her, clawing at her, urging her to give in. It was true, wasn't it? She had felt it from the moment she entered this place, that same void, that same sense of emptiness. The Hollow had been calling her all along. It had been there in the whispers, in the growls, in the visions of her lost friends. It had always been there, waiting for her to accept it.

But Eleanor knew, deep down, that if she gave in—if she allowed herself to become part of it—she would lose everything. She would lose Theo, Dapo, Ugochi, and herself. The Hollow would take everything from her. She would become nothing but a shadow, a reflection of the darkness, forever lost in its grasp.

"I will never join you," she said, her voice stronger now, cutting through the emptiness. "You don't own me."

The figure's smile widened, the darkness around it intensifying. "You already are mine," it hissed, its voice a low growl that sent shivers through her body. "You just don't realize it yet."

For a moment, Eleanor stood frozen, the weight of its words sinking into her skin like poison. The shadows pressed in around her, their fingers curling around her thoughts, threatening to pull her under. But she didn't give in. She wouldn't.

With a sudden surge of will, she took a step forward, her body shaking with the effort. The figure recoiled as if it were repelled by her movement, its form flickering, uncertain. Eleanor's heart raced, the pulse of her own fear mingling with the rhythm of the Hollow's whispers. The rift in front of her seemed to shudder, as though it, too, was uncertain of what would happen next.

Eleanor clenched her fist, feeling the jagged stone dig into her palm. She had come this far. She had fought so hard. She wouldn't let it all end here, not like this, not consumed by the Hollow's lies.

"I am not yours," she repeated, her voice firm, her chest rising and falling with each breath. "I belong to myself. I belong to the people I love. And I will not let you take that from me."

The figure let out a low, guttural laugh, its eyes flashing with anger. "You think you can fight me?" it sneered. "You think you can fight what is inside you? The Hollow is part of you, Eleanor. You are already mine."

But as the figure stepped forward, Eleanor raised the jagged stone high, and with all the strength she had left, she hurled it toward the darkness. The stone flew through the air, cutting through the shadows, and struck the figure in the chest. It let out a howl of rage, its form beginning to fragment, splintering like glass.

For a moment, the world held its breath.

And then, the rift before her exploded in a burst of blinding light.

The darkness recoiled, screeching in fury as the light pierced through it, scattering the shadows like dust in the wind. Eleanor closed her eyes against the brilliance, feeling the warmth of it flood over her, pushing the darkness back, back into the void from which it had come. She could feel the Hollow's presence weakening, its grip on her slowly loosening, fading.

And for the first time in what felt like forever, Eleanor felt the weight of the abyss lift.

18

Fragments of the Fallen

The blinding light was gone.

Eleanor stood motionless, her heart still hammering in her chest, the remnants of the rift swirling around her like smoke. The world seemed to hold its breath. The air was thick, almost oppressive, but there was something in it now—a shift, a subtle change that whispered of possibility. She couldn't yet tell if it was hope or something else—something far more dangerous.

She wiped her brow, the cold sweat mingling with the dirt on her face. Her body ached with exhaustion, her limbs heavy from the strain of everything she had been through. Yet there was a strange clarity in her mind now, as though the fog had lifted, if only for a moment. The Hollow's suffocating presence had faltered, its grip weakening, but she knew this wasn't over. Not yet. It was far from over.

The light that had filled the cavern had faded into nothingness, leaving her standing at the center of a vast, empty expanse.

There were no walls, no shadows, no rift—just an endless stretch of grey, an eerie, unsettling stillness that seemed to pull at her very soul. She could feel the weight of it, the way the air seemed to shift with each breath, as if the world was waiting for something. For her, maybe.

"Dapo?" Her voice cracked in the silence, her words a soft whisper that seemed to get lost in the emptiness. The name tasted bitter on her tongue, a reminder of all the moments they had lost, of all the things that had been torn from them both. But she needed to hear it, needed to know if he was still out there, somewhere, anywhere.

There was no answer.

Her pulse quickened. Was he gone? Had she failed him, too? The thought was like a fist to the gut, squeezing the air from her lungs. She couldn't afford to lose anyone else. Not after everything she'd been through. Not after all the sacrifices they had made.

She closed her eyes, trying to calm her mind, trying to remember the words he had spoken to her, the warmth of his voice that had been a lifeline in the darkness. "Don't give up. Don't let the Hollow define you." The memory of his words filled her, a spark of something pure and real in the midst of all this chaos. She had fought for this. She had fought for him.

But now, standing in the emptiness, she wasn't so sure anymore. The pull of the darkness was still there, faint but insistent, like the distant hum of a machine that had never stopped running. She could feel it. The Hollow was still with her. Still in her.

The ground beneath her feet trembled, the air around her humming with an energy she couldn't place. Eleanor took a cautious step forward, her eyes scanning the void. Nothing moved. There were no sounds, no signs of life. She was alone.

For a moment, she thought of turning back. Of finding the rift, finding the way out. But the thought was immediately followed by another—what if there was no way out? What if this place was all there was now? What if she had fallen too deep to ever truly escape?

Her thoughts were interrupted by a sound. A soft whisper, so faint that she almost didn't hear it.

"Eleanor..."

She froze, every muscle in her body locking in place. The voice was soft, familiar, almost too soft, like it was coming from deep within her own mind.

"Dapo?" she whispered, hope igniting in her chest like a flame in the dark. She strained her ears, listening for any other sound.

"Eleanor..." The voice came again, closer now, as though it were circling around her, wrapping itself around her thoughts.

She spun around, her pulse spiking. There was nothing there— just the same endless void stretching out in all directions. The darkness was thick and suffocating, but there was no rift, no figure, no light. Only silence.

But then, it came again.

"Eleanor..."

This time, the voice was unmistakable. She recognized it. She knew it. It was Dapo's voice, clear and raw, but laced with something else—something that sent a shiver crawling up her spine. It was not just a voice calling out to her. It was a warning.

"No!" Eleanor's breath hitched. "No, no, no!" She spun around again, panic rising like a storm within her. She had to find him. She couldn't lose him. She couldn't lose everything they had fought for.

But the voice continued, growing louder, coming from all directions now. "Eleanor..."

She clasped her hands to her ears, her eyes wide, the tears welling up before she could stop them. Her mind raced, torn between fear and an overwhelming need to reach him.

But then, just as suddenly as the voice had appeared, it was gone. The silence returned.

Eleanor's chest heaved with the weight of her breath. She was shaking now, her whole body trembling with a mixture of fear, exhaustion, and disbelief.

And then she heard something else.

Footsteps.

Slow. Methodical. Heavy.

Eleanor's head snapped in the direction of the sound, her heart leaping into her throat. She was no longer alone.

The footsteps grew louder, closer, each one sending ripples of fear through her. Whoever—whatever—was coming toward her was moving with purpose. The hairs on the back of her neck stood on end, her body frozen in place, as though the very presence of this new entity was enough to paralyze her.

And then, from the edge of her vision, a figure emerged.

At first, it was a blur, a shadow moving in the periphery, but as it stepped into the space before her, Eleanor's breath caught in her throat.

It was him.

It was Dapo.

But it wasn't.

The figure stood before her, tall and imposing, its features obscured by the swirling shadows that clung to it like a shroud. Eleanor's heart skipped a beat. She knew that face. She had memorized every inch of it—the curve of his jaw, the way his eyes softened when he smiled. She knew the sound of his laugh, the warmth of his touch. But now, all of that was gone.

The figure before her was a hollow shell of the man she had once known. His skin was ashen, his eyes dark pits, and his lips were twisted in an eerie, almost mocking smile. There was no warmth in his presence, no familiarity, just an overwhelming coldness that seemed to seep into her very bones.

"Dapo?" she whispered, her voice trembling with disbelief. She could hardly bring herself to say his name.

The figure's smile widened.

"Eleanor..." The voice, unmistakably his, echoed in her ears. But there was something wrong with it. Something off. The warmth was gone.

Eleanor took a step back, her breath coming in ragged bursts. "No... no, this isn't you," she whispered.

The figure tilted its head, its eyes never leaving hers.

"No? But I am," it said, the voice dripping with something cruel, something unrecognizable. "I am what you made me. I am everything you let me become."

Eleanor's knees buckled, her heart racing as the weight of those words crushed down on her. This wasn't him. It couldn't be.

"Dapo," she repeated, her voice now rising in desperation.

"Please, I need you. Come back to me. You're not lost. You're not gone."

The figure took a step toward her, its footsteps echoing in the hollow silence, each one carrying an unsettling weight.

"But I am gone, Eleanor," it said softly. "I've always been gone. Don't you see? You let me go. You didn't save me. You couldn't."

"No!" she cried, stepping back again, her hands raised as if to ward off the apparition. "That's not true. You're here. You're real. I won't lose you!"

The figure's smile faded into something darker, more predatory. "You can't save me, Eleanor. You can't save anyone."

It was then that she realized the truth. This wasn't Dapo. Not anymore. This was the Hollow, wearing his face. The Hollow had already consumed him, and now it was showing her the destruction it had wrought.

A chill settled deep within her chest, and for the first time, Eleanor felt her legs give way. She crumpled to the ground, her mind reeling as the weight of everything she had lost came crashing down.

She had tried to save them. She had tried to save him. But maybe it was too late.

The shadows closed in. The figure loomed over her, a specter of everything she feared, everything she had failed to protect.

And then, as the darkness closed in around her, she heard it again.

"Eleanor."

Her heart skipped a beat, and she looked up. The voice was different this time—clear, strong, and full of life.

"Eleanor..."

She looked up.

It was Dapo.

19

The Flicker of Hope

Eleanor's eyes widened in disbelief. The figure standing before her was no longer a shadow of Dapo, no longer the twisted, hollow mockery of the man she loved. This was him. Real. Alive. The warmth of his gaze reached out to her, and for a moment, she could hardly breathe, the words stuck in her throat.

"Dapo?" she whispered, her voice trembling. She couldn't believe what she was seeing. Couldn't believe that after everything, after the darkness, after the rift, he was standing here in front of her.

Dapo's eyes locked onto hers, and in that moment, all the fear, all the uncertainty that had plagued her since she entered the Hollow seemed to dissipate. He looked different—his features were more defined, sharper—but the essence of who he was remained the same. The depth in his eyes, the steady, unwavering presence he always carried.

"Yes, Eleanor," he said, his voice low and rich with emotion, "it's me."

The words struck her like a wave crashing over rocks. She was on her feet before she even realized it, her body moving on instinct, propelled by the need to be close to him. She stumbled, her legs weak from the emotional whirlwind, but somehow, she made it to him, her arms reaching out.

She collided with his chest, the sudden contact overwhelming her senses. The smell of his skin—the faint scent of cedar and earth—was so familiar, so real. Her hands gripped his shirt tightly, as if afraid to let go, as if he might vanish the moment she stopped holding on.

"Dapo..." Her voice broke on his name, her heart racing. "You're really here. You're... you're alive. I thought—" She stopped, her words choking her. She couldn't say it. Couldn't voice the fear that had plagued her heart for so long: that she had lost him forever.

"I'm here," Dapo said softly, his hands gently cupping her face. "I'm right here. You're not alone."

Eleanor closed her eyes at his touch, the warmth of his hands grounding her, pulling her back from the edge of the abyss she had been teetering on. She pressed her forehead against his chest, breathing him in, trying to believe that this was real. That this wasn't some cruel trick of the Hollow.

But the moment was fleeting, fragile.

As they stood there, wrapped in each other's arms, a subtle, unsettling chill crept into the air. The world around them was still empty, the vast, grey expanse stretching endlessly in every direction. For all the comfort that Dapo's presence gave her, the eerie silence that had once filled the cavern now seemed to pulse with an even more sinister energy.

Dapo's fingers brushed through her hair, his touch tender but urgent.

"We need to go," he said quietly, his voice edged with something Eleanor couldn't place. "We don't have much time."

Eleanor pulled back slightly, her brow furrowing. "Go? Where?"

He looked at her, his eyes dark with something she couldn't name—fear, maybe, or something worse. "The Hollow is still here, Eleanor. It's still coming. We can't stay here. We need to get out. We need to leave before it finds us."

Eleanor's heart skipped a beat. The Hollow. Of course. How could she have forgotten? It was everywhere. It was in the air, in the earth, in her very thoughts. She felt the weight of it again—the way the very space around them seemed to close in, suffocating her, pressing down with an invisible force. It had never truly left her. Not really.

"Then how do we leave?" she asked, her voice shaking. "How do we escape this place? How do we escape the Hollow?"

Dapo's expression grew more somber, more distant. He looked past her, his eyes unfocused for a moment, as though he was seeing something she couldn't.

"I don't know," he murmured, his words heavy. "But we can't stay. The longer we're here, the stronger the Hollow gets. We'll lose ourselves."

Eleanor swallowed hard, her throat dry. The Hollow had already taken so much. It had taken Theo. It had taken Ugochi. She had been so close to losing Dapo, too. The thought made her stomach twist.

"But—" Eleanor began, her voice faltering, "We can't just leave. I—I can't just leave without understanding. I need to know what's happening. I need to know how to stop it. If we leave now, what happens to the others? What happens to everyone we've lost?"

Dapo looked down, his face tight with pain. "I wish I knew, Eleanor," he said, his voice strained. "I wish I had all the answers. But this place—this thing—it's not something we can fight with force or reason. It's ancient. It's a part of the world, a part of everything. And the more we stay here, the more it will consume us. If we don't leave, we'll become a part of it. We'll become them."

Eleanor's stomach churned at the thought. The Hollow had already taken so many—her friends, her family, her sanity. The idea of becoming one of those twisted, hollow versions of the people she loved was too much to bear. She shuddered, her hands trembling as she gripped Dapo tighter.

"We have to leave, then," she said, her voice tight with resolve. "We have to find a way out."

Dapo nodded, his expression still grim. He looked over his shoulder, his gaze scanning the endless, empty landscape that stretched before them. "There's only one way, Eleanor. And it's not going to be easy."

Eleanor furrowed her brow. "What do you mean?"

Dapo's lips pressed into a thin line, his jaw tightening as he looked at her. "The Hollow doesn't just exist in this place. It exists in us, in everything we are, in everything we've ever known. It's like a parasite, feeding off of our fear, our pain, our memories. The only way to truly escape it is to sever that connection. To stop running from it."

Eleanor's mind raced. "What do you mean by 'sever the connection'? How do we do that?"

Dapo shook his head slowly. "I don't know if we can. I don't know if there's anything left of us that hasn't already been touched by it. But if we don't try, we'll lose everything. The Hollow will consume us. Everything we are, everything we've been, will be gone."

Eleanor's heart thudded painfully in her chest. She could feel the weight of his words settling over her like a shroud. The Hollow wasn't just a place. It was an all-encompassing force, a darkness that had invaded every corner of her life, twisting it, shaping it into something unrecognizable.

And yet, despite everything, despite the fear that gripped her insides, she knew he was right. They had to try. They had to find a way to escape it, or they would lose everything.

"We'll figure it out," she said firmly, more to herself than to Dapo. "We have to."

Dapo looked at her with something close to admiration, the faintest flicker of hope in his eyes. "We will. Together."

A gust of cold air swept through the space, and Eleanor's eyes flickered toward the source of the movement. In the distance, a shadow moved—a dark silhouette against the grey backdrop. It was more than a figure this time. It was a presence, a feeling. Something was watching them. Something was coming.

Dapo stiffened. His hand shot out to grab Eleanor's arm, pulling her closer. "We have to move now. They're coming."

Eleanor's heart lurched in her chest. They?

The air around them shifted again, this time with a sharp crackle of energy. The ground trembled underfoot. The Hollow was awakening, and it wasn't about to let them go.

"Run," Dapo commanded, his voice urgent.

Without hesitation, Eleanor turned and sprinted, Dapo beside her, both of them moving toward the only thing they knew: the distant, faint flicker of light that appeared in the far-off horizon.

The shadows behind them grew darker, stretching out like tendrils, reaching toward them with a hunger that seemed insatiable. The ground beneath their feet seemed to shift, making every step feel like an effort, like the earth itself was trying to swallow them.

But Eleanor couldn't stop. She couldn't slow down. Not now. Not when they were so close.

She could hear the whispers of the Hollow behind them, like thousands of voices murmuring at once, urging her to stop. To give in. To accept her fate. But she ignored it. She clenched her teeth and pushed forward, knowing that if she stopped now, if she looked back, she would be lost.

Dapo's hand tightened on hers, pulling her faster, urging her forward. The light grew brighter with every step. They were getting closer.

And for the first time in what felt like an eternity, Eleanor allowed herself to believe in the impossible.

20

Into the Light

Eleanor's heart thundered in her chest, every beat reverberating in her skull. Her breath came in ragged gasps as she ran, the cold air biting at her skin, sharp like the edge of a blade. Dapo was beside her, his grip tight on her hand, pulling her along with a desperation she could feel in the tremor of his fingers. The flicker of light ahead of them was their only guide, a promise, fragile and fleeting, in the suffocating darkness that surrounded them.

They didn't look back. They couldn't.

Every step felt like an eternity. The ground beneath them seemed to shift, pulling at their feet as though the earth itself was resisting their escape. The air grew heavier, thick with the oppressive weight of the Hollow, suffocating them with each breath they took. The light, distant as it was, seemed to pulse in rhythm with their frantic heartbeats, growing brighter and dimmer, as though it was teasing them, daring them to reach it.

Eleanor's thoughts were a blur. All that mattered now was getting to that light. Getting out of this nightmare.

"Don't stop," Dapo's voice was hoarse, laced with urgency, as he tugged her forward, his gaze fixed on the flickering light in the distance. "We can't stop. We can't let it catch us."

Eleanor's legs burned, her body protesting the relentless pace, but she pushed forward, the sound of her shoes slapping against the ground drowning out everything else. The Hollow was behind them, she could feel it. Like a presence, a cold breath on the back of her neck, creeping closer with every passing second. The whispers, the voices of the Hollow, grew louder in her ears, distorted and alien, like a thousand twisted souls speaking at once.

Stop... turn around...

Her pulse quickened. She couldn't let it pull her back. Not now. Not after everything.

"We're almost there," Dapo said, his voice strained but determined. He didn't look at her, but she could feel the intensity in his words. It was as if he, too, could feel the weight of the darkness bearing down on them. The Hollow was closing in, its tendrils reaching out, stretching toward them like the fingers of a monstrous hand, clawing at their heels.

Please... don't stop...

It was the voice again. The same haunting whisper that had

plagued her since the moment she set foot in this place. A voice, or perhaps many voices, echoing through the void. Eleanor tried to block them out, to focus on the flicker of light ahead. But the closer they got, the louder the voices became.

Turn around...

"No," Eleanor whispered through clenched teeth, shaking her head as if to clear the voices from her mind. "I won't listen to you."

But the Hollow didn't care. It didn't listen. It only took. It only consumed.

"Dapo," she gasped, her breath coming in ragged bursts. "It's getting closer. It's pulling us in. I can feel it."

"I know," he said grimly, his grip tightening on her hand. "I can feel it too. But we can't stop. We can't give in."

They ran faster, but it wasn't enough. The light was still too far away. Too distant. They needed to reach it. They needed to escape.

A scream tore through the air, sharp and piercing. Eleanor froze for a split second, her heart leaping into her throat.

"Did you hear that?" she gasped, her voice trembling with fear.

Dapo's eyes flashed to her, his face pale, eyes wide. "Keep running. Don't stop."

But Eleanor could see it. A figure in the distance, barely visible through the haze of the darkened air, a shadow moving with unnatural speed. It was coming toward them.

"No…" she whispered, the realization dawning on her like a weight crushing her chest. The figure was getting closer, faster, its form flickering in and out of existence like a half-formed nightmare. It was no longer just a shadow—it was something real. Something that wanted to drag them back.

The Hollow.

It was right behind them.

Eleanor's pulse raced as the figure grew larger, more defined. It wasn't human. It was a creature made of darkness, its features shifting, constantly morphing like the fabric of the night itself. It had no face, no eyes, no mouth, but Eleanor could feel its gaze on her, could feel the weight of its presence as though it were clawing at her soul.

"We're almost there," Dapo said, his voice tight with fear, but there was no mistaking the urgency in it now. He tugged harder on her hand, pulling her forward, but Eleanor couldn't tear her eyes away from the thing that was following them. The Hollow was closing in, its form becoming more tangible with each passing second.

"Dapo!" Eleanor screamed, her voice rising in panic. "It's right there! We can't outrun it! We can't—"

"We can!" Dapo roared, his voice raw with determination. "We can! Just trust me!"

And just like that, the words seemed to cut through the fog of fear that had clouded her mind. Trust him. She had to trust him. She had trusted him once before, in the darkest moments of their journey, and it had kept them alive. She had to trust him now, with everything she had.

Without another word, she gripped his hand tighter, her pace quickening, her legs screaming in protest. The light in the distance flickered again, almost as if it were beckoning them. She couldn't see it clearly, but she could feel it. It was a door, a way out. A lifeline. And if she didn't reach it soon, they would be lost.

Her breath burned in her lungs, her muscles screaming for mercy, but she kept running. The Hollow was close now, its form growing clearer, its presence suffocating, the air thickening with its weight. Eleanor could hear its whispers now, louder than ever, a cacophony of voices filling her ears.

Come back... You belong with us...

"No!" she cried, her voice breaking. "I won't go back. I won't let you take me."

But the Hollow didn't care. It was patient. It would wait. It would chase them until the very end.

Dapo's grip tightened on her hand, his arm swinging around

her waist as he pulled her forward, their bodies moving in sync, a single force driving them toward the light. They couldn't stop. Not now.

The air around them pulsed with a low hum, the ground trembling beneath their feet as the Hollow grew closer, its monstrous form closing in. Eleanor glanced back, her heart sinking as she saw the full extent of the nightmare chasing them. The thing was no longer a shadow. It was a creature of pure darkness, a mass of writhing tendrils and shifting forms that seemed to stretch forever, its presence suffocating, its movements erratic. It was alive. And it was hungry.

The ground buckled beneath their feet, and for a moment, Eleanor thought they might fall, that they might be dragged back into the depths of the Hollow. But Dapo didn't hesitate. He pulled her forward, his face set in grim determination, his eyes locked on the light.

They were so close now. So close.

The air around them crackled with energy, a force like static filling the space. The light flickered again, brighter this time, as though it had heard their cries, as though it were reaching out to them. But the Hollow wasn't done. It wasn't going to let them go without a fight.

Suddenly, the creature lunged, its tendrils reaching out, grasping for them. Eleanor screamed, but Dapo didn't stop. He didn't flinch. He kept pulling her forward, faster now, as the Hollow's tendrils scraped the ground, slithering toward them like serpents. The world around them seemed to twist, to bend under the weight of the darkness, but the light ahead—the light—was still there, still shining.

And then, with a final burst of energy, they reached it.

The light exploded around them, a wave of blinding brilliance that engulfed them both. Eleanor gasped, her body jerking as though it were being pulled from the very fabric of the Hollow. The tendrils reached out one last time, but they were too slow. The light closed in around them, encasing them in warmth, in protection.

Eleanor's vision blurred, her body weightless as if floating in an ocean of light. The Hollow's whispers faded into nothingness, the darkness retreating, leaving only the light. The light that pulled her, that saved her.

And then—nothing.

Silence.

When Eleanor opened her eyes, she was no longer running. The ground beneath her was solid, and the air was no longer thick and suffocating. She blinked, her surroundings coming into focus. She was back. Back where it all began.

Dapo stood beside her, breathing heavily, his expression just as dazed as hers. They were standing in the middle of a familiar, open space. The quiet, the stillness—everything felt so... real. She glanced around, her heart pounding in her chest. The

Hollow was gone. The darkness had faded.

They were free.

Dapo turned to her, his face softening into a smile. "We made it," he whispered, his voice thick with emotion.

Eleanor smiled, the weight

21

Echoes of the Past

Eleanor stood still, her breath still caught in her throat. The air around her was clean, crisp, and real. No longer was it thick with the weight of the Hollow, no longer suffocating her every breath. But even as she breathed in the fresh air, there was something... wrong. Something unsettled in the pit of her stomach.

Dapo's hand was still clutching hers, warm and steady, but there was a tension in his grip that hadn't been there before. Eleanor glanced at him, trying to make sense of the stillness that enveloped them. He was staring ahead, his eyes distant, locked on something she couldn't see, as though trying to comprehend the same feeling that gnawed at her.

"We're out," she whispered, more to herself than to him.

"Yes," he replied quietly, though his voice lacked the triumph she had expected. "But the question is... where are we?"

Eleanor blinked. She hadn't considered that. They had escaped the Hollow, but in doing so, they had left behind the world they knew—the world they had fought so hard to return to. The world where people had died, where memories had been twisted and broken. The place they had both been lost in for so long.

She turned slowly, looking at their surroundings. The place they stood seemed strangely familiar, yet deeply foreign at the same time. The ground beneath her feet was soft and damp, not like the cracked, dry earth of the Hollow, but like fresh, untouched soil. There were trees around them—tall, thick-barked trees with leaves that shimmered faintly in the twilight. It was a forest, but it wasn't the forest they had known. This place felt... unreal. Like it was both a memory and a dream.

"Where are we, Dapo?" Eleanor asked, her voice trembling, as though asking the question would bring her closer to an answer.

Dapo took a step forward, his expression unreadable. "I don't know. But I don't like it."

Eleanor felt a chill creep down her spine. She had never heard Dapo's voice like that—low, tense, filled with an unfamiliar edge. The certainty in his tone unsettled her. She had always trusted him. But this place, this... dreamscape, was making even him uneasy.

"We need to keep moving," he said after a long pause, pulling her gently by the arm. "Stay close."

Eleanor nodded, her heart racing, though she couldn't decide if it was from fear or from the unsettling sense of déjà vu that gripped her every step. The trees around them were eerily silent. There were no birds, no sounds of wildlife. Just the rustle of the leaves in the wind, and the steady beat of their own footsteps as they moved deeper into the forest.

As they walked, the silence began to grow heavier. It was the kind of silence that presses against you, filling the empty space, growing thicker and thicker until you can almost feel it, like a weight on your chest. The light from the setting sun filtered weakly through the branches above, casting long, thin shadows on the forest floor, giving everything a ghostly, ethereal quality. Eleanor kept glancing over her shoulder, half-expecting to see something lurking behind them, watching them from the dark.

Suddenly, a sharp sound broke through the silence—a distant rustling. Eleanor froze, her pulse jumping in her throat. Dapo's hand tightened around hers.

"Did you hear that?" she whispered, her voice barely audible.

Dapo nodded, his jaw clenched. "Stay behind me."

Before Eleanor could protest, Dapo pulled ahead, guiding her through the trees with a speed and purpose that unsettled her. She kept pace with him, but every fiber of her being screamed to stop, to turn back, to find the source of the sound. But there was something in the air now—an almost tangible presence, pressing in on them from all sides. It felt... wrong.

The forest, once silent, now seemed to hum with the echoes of something not quite human. She could feel eyes on them—hundreds, thousands of eyes, hidden deep within the shadows. Watching. Waiting.

They turned a corner, and Eleanor's breath caught in her throat. There, standing in the middle of a clearing, was something that stopped her dead in her tracks. It was an altar—old and weathered, made of stone, covered in moss and vines. But what made her blood run cold was the figure standing before it.

A woman. Tall, with long, black hair that shimmered in the dim light. She was dressed in white robes that seemed to glow faintly in the growing darkness. But what terrified Eleanor wasn't her beauty, or the ethereal way she stood, almost floating above the ground. It was her eyes—cold, hollow, endless pits of darkness, eyes that seemed to swallow everything around them.

Dapo stopped beside her, his posture stiffening. "We shouldn't be here," he muttered under his breath. "We need to go."

But Eleanor couldn't move. She was rooted to the spot, her legs locked in place. The figure turned slowly, her eyes locking onto Eleanor's with a predatory calmness that made her stomach twist. The woman's lips parted in a slow, chilling smile.

"I see you've returned," the woman said, her voice a low, melodic whisper, as though the words were not meant for this world at all.

Eleanor's throat tightened, her heart pounding in her chest. "Who... who are you?"

The woman stepped closer, the air growing colder with every movement she made. "I am the one who watches. I am the echo of what you left behind."

The words struck Eleanor like a bolt of lightning. She stepped back, her mind racing. Echo of what they left behind? What did that mean? They had left the Hollow, but this place—it felt wrong, as though it was a reflection of their fears, their memories twisted into something more sinister.

Dapo's voice broke through her thoughts, sharp and urgent. "Eleanor, get back!"

But it was too late. The woman's eyes glinted with dark amusement as she reached out, her hand stretching unnaturally long, fingers twisting like vines. She made no sound, no sudden movement, but Eleanor felt her mind begin to unravel in the woman's gaze.

"This is where it all begins," the woman intoned, her voice wrapping around Eleanor like a silk rope, suffocating her. "The Hollow didn't leave you. It was never truly gone. It was just waiting—waiting for you to return."

Eleanor gasped, her chest tightening, but she couldn't pull her eyes away from the woman. The world around her began to blur, the forest around her seeming to bend and twist. The trees seemed to warp, the ground shifting beneath her feet.

"Stop," Dapo said, his voice strained, pulling her away. "You have to fight it, Eleanor. Don't let it take you."

But the words barely reached her. She felt a presence—dark, suffocating, crawling into her skin. The woman's words were wrapping around her mind, pulling at the fragile threads of her sanity.

"You've been marked," the woman whispered. "You can't escape what you are. You can't escape the Hollow. It's in your blood now. You belong to it."

"No..." Eleanor breathed, trying to tear her gaze away, but it was as if her body no longer obeyed her. She could feel the darkness seeping into her mind, cold tendrils curling around her thoughts. Her body went rigid, every muscle frozen in place as the woman's smile stretched wider, her eyes swallowing Eleanor whole.

But then—just as suddenly as it had begun—Dapo was there, grabbing her by the shoulders and pulling her away. The woman's laugh echoed in the distance, but it was distant now. Faint.

Eleanor's vision blurred as Dapo yanked her backward, away from the altar, away from the woman. The dark presence that had threatened to swallow her retreated like mist, dissipating into the air.

"Eleanor," Dapo said, his voice raw, desperate. "You need to wake up. Come on, please."

Eleanor shook her head, her breath ragged. Her mind felt foggy, disjointed. "What... what was that? Who was she?"

"I don't know," Dapo said quickly, his voice strained with emotion. "But we need to leave. Now. This place—it's not just a forest. It's part of the Hollow. It's feeding off of us. We can't stay here."

Eleanor blinked, trying to clear her head, but the woman's words echoed in her mind.

You belong to it.

"Dapo," she said, her voice weak, her throat tight. "What if we can't escape? What if the Hollow isn't gone? What if it's still here—inside us?"

Dapo's eyes flickered with a sorrow she hadn't seen before. "We fight it," he said, his voice hoarse. "Together."

But even as he said the words, Eleanor couldn't help but wonder if they were already too late.

22

The Veil of Shadows

The storm had passed, leaving the world cloaked in a heavy, unnatural stillness. Eleanor stood in the middle of the clearing, surrounded by the remnants of the battle—the scorched earth, the uprooted trees, the lingering echoes of a darkness that had once threatened to consume everything in its path. The air smelled faintly of burning wood, mingled with the damp scent of the forest's moist soil. But beneath the tangible remnants of destruction, there was an unsettling quiet—a silence that seemed too deep, too profound, as though the world itself were holding its breath.

Eleanor could feel it, the weight of that silence pressing in on her, wrapping around her like a heavy cloak. The Hollow was gone. Or so she had believed. But something was wrong. Deep down, she could sense that the battle had not truly ended. The storm had subsided, yes, but the peace was fragile. And the darkness? It still lingered at the edge of her mind, like a shadow that refused to fade, no matter how brightly the light tried to shine.

Dapo's voice cut through her thoughts, soft yet steady, like a lifeline. "Eleanor, are you all right?"

She turned to face him, forcing a smile, but the concern in his eyes made her heart twist. He could see it, too—the fear, the doubt, the weight of an invisible presence that hung over them. Dapo was a man of few words, but his silence spoke volumes. He had been her rock, her constant companion through every storm, but even he couldn't shake the feeling that something was wrong.

"I'm fine," she replied, her voice betraying her with its unsteady tremor. "I just... I don't know. I can still feel it, Dapo. The Hollow. It's not gone. Not really."

Dapo stepped closer, his expression darkening as he glanced around the clearing, his sharp eyes scanning the shadows. "It's quiet. Too quiet. I feel it too. But you defeated it. You were strong enough to face it. Don't doubt that."

"I'm not doubting that," Eleanor whispered, her voice tight. "But what if I'm not done yet? What if the Hollow didn't leave? What if it's... still inside me?"

The words hung between them, heavier than any storm. Eleanor's breath caught in her throat as she swallowed hard, trying to push the dread back down, but it was like trying to hold back an ocean with a single hand. The Hollow had been more than just a force of darkness. It had been a part of her, feeding off her fears, her insecurities, her own self-doubt. And now, in the aftermath of their battle, it was like a lingering echo, a reminder that it had never truly gone away.

Dapo reached out, his hand gently brushing her shoulder, grounding her with his touch. "You're not alone in this, Eleanor. You've never been. Whatever it is, we'll face it together. You've already beaten it once. You can do it again."

She wanted to believe him. She wanted to believe that the

Hollow was gone for good, that the peace they had fought for was finally within reach. But as her eyes drifted across the clearing, a sudden unease settled deep in her bones. Something was wrong. And the longer she stood there, the more she felt it—a presence, lurking just beyond the edge of her perception, watching, waiting.

Suddenly, a sharp crack echoed through the stillness, and Eleanor froze. It came from the woods, a sound like a branch snapping underfoot, followed by a low, guttural growl. Her heart skipped a beat. The Hollow? Or something worse?

"Did you hear that?" she whispered, her voice barely audible. Dapo nodded, his body tensing, every muscle coiled in anticipation. He looked around, his hand instinctively moving toward the knife at his belt.

"I did," he said quietly. "Stay close."

Eleanor felt a chill crawl up her spine. The Hollow had been banished, yes, but its legacy was not easily erased. It was like a poison in her veins, and as the growl echoed through the trees again, she knew that the Hollow wasn't finished with her. Not yet.

Dapo took a step forward, his movements fluid and quiet. He glanced back at Eleanor, his eyes flickering with determination. "Stay here. Keep your distance. I'll investigate."

"No." Eleanor's voice was firm, the fear in her chest giving way to something else—something fierce. "I'm not staying behind. We face this together."

Without waiting for his reply, she moved to his side, her steps steady, her heart pounding in her ears. She couldn't let the fear control her, not again. Not after everything they had been through. If the Hollow was coming back, then she would fight it with everything she had left. She *would* face it.

They moved through the forest together, their footsteps muffled by the thick carpet of fallen leaves. The growl grew louder, closer, a low rumbling that seemed to reverberate through the ground beneath their feet. Eleanor's breath quickened, and she fought to steady herself, to push aside the panic that threatened to rise. She could do this. She *had* to.

Suddenly, Dapo stopped, his body tense. "There," he whispered, pointing to a shadow that moved between the trees. It was large, hulking, and vaguely human in shape—but there was something wrong with it, something twisted. The air seemed to ripple around it, the very fabric of reality warping in its presence.

Eleanor's stomach twisted with dread, but she refused to back down. She stepped forward, her eyes locked on the figure. "What is that?"

Dapo's expression was grim. "I don't know. But it's not the Hollow. It's something else."

The figure moved again, and for a moment, Eleanor thought she saw something glimmer in the dark—a pair of eyes, glowing faintly in the shadows. And then, as if it had heard her thoughts, it stepped into the light, revealing itself fully.

It wasn't a man. It wasn't human at all. The creature that stood before them was a grotesque, misshapen thing—its skin pale and slick, like that of a fish, its eyes wide and unblinking, glowing with an unnatural light. Its limbs were long and spindly, its hands ending in sharp claws that gleamed in the dim light. Its mouth was wide, jagged teeth lining the edges of its jaw.

Eleanor's breath caught in her throat. The Hollow had a shape, a form, but this... this was something else entirely. Something worse.

"What is that?" she breathed again, her voice shaking.

"I don't know," Dapo said, his tone tight. "But we need to take it down. Now."

The creature let out a low hiss, its head swiveling to fixate on them, its eyes burning with malevolent intent. It began to move toward them, its claws scraping against the forest floor, a sound that sent chills down Eleanor's spine.

In that moment, everything felt unreal—like the world had shifted, and they were no longer part of the same reality. The creature was upon them in an instant, its movements swift and fluid, faster than anything Eleanor had ever seen.

Dapo reacted first, his knife flashing as he lunged at the creature, aiming for its throat. But the creature was too quick. It twisted, its claws slicing through the air in a blur, narrowly missing Dapo's outstretched arm. Eleanor gasped, but she didn't hesitate. She reached for the dagger at her side, her fingers trembling as she gripped it tightly.

The battle was on.

The creature's speed was overwhelming. It seemed to be everywhere at once—dodging, attacking, moving with a grace that was almost impossible for a human to match. Dapo parried a strike, narrowly avoiding the creature's claws, but it was clear they were outmatched. The thing was stronger, faster, and seemingly unkillable.

Eleanor's heart pounded in her chest as she struggled to keep up, her thoughts a whirlwind of fear and determination. They couldn't let it win. They couldn't let it take them, not when they had come so far. But with every swing of her blade, every thrust of her dagger, the creature simply danced out of the way, its eerie eyes never leaving hers.

Desperation clawed at her chest. She couldn't keep this up

forever. And then, just as the creature lunged at Dapo with a vicious snarl, Eleanor saw her chance. The creature's claws were exposed, its guard momentarily down. Without thinking, she acted.

She dove forward, her dagger raised high, and drove it deep into the creature's side.

For a moment, time seemed to stop. The creature froze, its glowing eyes flickering with shock and pain. And then, with a deafening screech, it collapsed to the ground, its form twitching violently as it spasmed and writhed.

Eleanor stood over it, her breath ragged, her heart thundering in her chest. The creature was dying. Slowly, it crumbled, its unnatural form fading away like mist, leaving only the faintest traces of its presence behind.

As silence fell over the clearing, Eleanor collapsed to her knees, her body shaking with exhaustion, relief, and a lingering fear that refused to let go. She had fought it, and she had won. But the battle wasn't over yet.

She could still feel the Hollow. Still feel the shadows.

And she knew, deep down, that the true fight was only just beginning.

23

The Edge of Madness

The forest had changed. The shadows were darker now, heavier, as if the trees themselves had drawn closer together, locking Eleanor and Dapo in a cage of branches and leaves. The stillness was unbearable, the silence so thick that every breath felt like a violation of the air around them. It was as if the world was holding its breath, waiting for something. Waiting for them.

Eleanor could feel it—the presence. The heavy, suffocating weight of it pressing down on her chest, the echo of the Hollow still lingering in her bones. She had fought it, had tried to outrun it, but the truth that the gatekeeper had spoken rang too loudly in her mind:

It is part of you. And it is coming for you.

Dapo's grip on her hand tightened, his knuckles white with the force of it. She glanced at him, her heart pounding in her chest, but his face was grim. He was just as afraid as she was. The certainty of the Hollow's return was too much for either of them to deny now.

"Dapo," Eleanor whispered, her voice trembling, "what do we do?"

He didn't answer immediately, his eyes scanning the darkness around them, looking for something, anything, that would offer a hint of safety. But the forest was empty, or so it seemed. The trees loomed like silent sentinels, their branches bending unnaturally in the wind, whispering something Eleanor couldn't quite make out.

Finally, Dapo turned to her, his face hard and resolute, but there was a flicker of something—something deep and unsettled—that she couldn't place. "We keep moving," he said, his voice barely above a whisper. "We can't stop. Not now."

Eleanor nodded, though her legs felt as though they were moving through quicksand. Every step she took felt like it pulled her deeper into a nightmare that she couldn't wake up from. She had to focus, had to remind herself that the Hollow was not a place. It wasn't an external thing. It was inside her. She had to fight it. But how? How could she fight something that lived inside her blood?

They walked in silence, their feet crunching softly against the forest floor, the only sound in the thick, oppressive air. With every step, Eleanor felt the weight of the world pressing on her more and more, the fear and uncertainty wrapping around her like a vice. She had no idea where they were going, no idea how to escape this place. The further they walked, the more it felt like they were walking in circles. The forest seemed to shift, the trees stretching and warping in strange ways, like the entire world was turning into a maze that they could never escape.

Suddenly, a sound—a crack of a branch snapping—cut through the silence. Eleanor froze, her breath catching in her throat. Dapo turned toward the sound, his body tense, his hand reaching for the knife at his side.

But nothing emerged from the trees. No creature. No figure. Just the eerie quiet of the forest. And yet, something felt different. The air felt thick now, charged with an energy she couldn't explain.

Another crack. This time closer.

Eleanor's pulse quickened. Her heart pounded in her ears as she glanced over her shoulder, but all she could see was darkness. She tried to push the rising panic from her mind, tried to hold on to the thin thread of reason that still tethered her to reality. But it was slipping. Slipping fast.

"Dapo," she whispered, her voice shaking. "Do you feel that?"

He didn't answer immediately. He just kept scanning the shadows, his jaw tight, his posture coiled, ready to spring.

Then, in the distance, something shifted. Something moved. A shadow in the darkness. Eleanor's breath caught in her throat as she took a step back, pulling Dapo closer.

"I saw it," she breathed. "I saw something."

Dapo's gaze hardened. "Stay close. Whatever it is, it's not real. We need to keep moving."

But even as he spoke, Eleanor could feel it—a presence. It was in the air, in the ground beneath their feet, in the weight of the silence that hung over them. She had felt it before—the Hollow. It was here. And this time, it wasn't just a whisper in the dark. It was real. It was alive.

"Dapo," she said, her voice cracking. "I don't think we can outrun it. I don't think we can escape."

He turned sharply toward her, his eyes flashing with something fierce. "We can, Eleanor. We just have to believe that we can."

But Eleanor wasn't so sure. The doubt that had been creeping in—the gnawing feeling that they were running in circles, that there was no way out—was taking root in her mind. What if Dapo was wrong? What if they had already crossed the point of no return? What if the Hollow had already claimed them, body and soul?

Another sound—closer this time. A snap of a twig, the rustle of leaves.

Eleanor's blood ran cold. The presence was closer now, and it was undeniable. She could feel it wrapping around her, a tight, suffocating grip. She wasn't sure where it had come from, or when it had started, but now, it was everywhere.

She stepped backward, a single, instinctive movement, but the ground was uneven, and her foot caught on a hidden root. Before she could stop herself, she fell, sprawling across the ground with a sharp gasp. Her breath was knocked out of her, and for a moment, she couldn't move. But the sensation of eyes watching her—dark, hungry eyes—was enough to get her back on her feet.

"Eleanor," Dapo called sharply, reaching for her, but she had already pushed herself up, panic flaring in her chest. She wasn't sure what was real anymore. The trees were shifting, the shadows were growing deeper, and the sounds—those sounds—seemed to grow louder, closer.

Then she heard it—a whisper. Faint at first, like the rustling of wind through the trees. But then, it grew louder, sharper, more distinct.

You can't run.

Eleanor's heart hammered in her chest as she spun around, her eyes wide, searching the darkness for the source of the voice. But there was nothing. Nothing but the shifting shadows and the oppressive silence.

You can't escape it. It's in you. It will always be in you.

"No," Eleanor whispered, shaking her head violently. "No, I won't let you in. I won't—"

Her words were cut off by a sudden force, a cold, bone-chilling pressure that slammed into her chest. The air around her grew dense, suffocating, as if the very atmosphere was trying to crush her. She gasped for breath, but it was as if the air had turned to stone, pressing in on her from all sides.

Dapo grabbed her arm, pulling her toward him. "Eleanor, we need to go! This place is twisting us! It's pulling us into it."

But Eleanor couldn't move. She couldn't think. The whispers were growing louder, a chorus of voices in her mind, telling her the same thing over and over.

You're not strong enough. You belong to it.

Tears welled up in Eleanor's eyes as the darkness around her thickened, swirling with the weight of every fear, every doubt, every piece of her soul that had been broken in the Hollow. It was here, inside her, just as the gatekeeper had said. The Hollow was never just a place. It was a part of her—of all of them. It was feeding off her fear, her despair. And now, it was winning.

"Dapo," she gasped, her voice breaking, her knees buckling beneath her as the weight of it overwhelmed her. "I can't... I can't fight it."

Dapo's face twisted with pain, his eyes filled with helplessness. He fell to his knees beside her, gripping her shoulders tightly as though willing her to look at him.

"You're not alone," he said, his voice rough, raw with emotion. "We're in this together, Eleanor. We've always been in this together."

But his words—his assurances—felt empty now. She could feel the Hollow's presence crawling through her veins, its tendrils digging deep, wrapping around her heart, suffocating her. She had tried to fight it, tried to push it out, but there was no escape.

She had known, deep down, that the Hollow would never truly let her go.

"You have to fight," Dapo whispered urgently, shaking her gently, his voice raw with fear. "Please, Eleanor. Fight it."

She wanted to—she wanted to fight. But the more she tried, the harder it became to breathe, to think, to even exist. She was slipping. And the more she slipped, the more she could feel it. The Hollow wasn't outside her anymore. It was part of her.

And as the darkness closed in around her, Eleanor couldn't shake the horrifying thought that maybe… maybe Dapo was wrong. Maybe there was no way out.

24

The Breaking Point

The ground beneath Eleanor's feet felt like it was shifting, as if the earth itself was slipping away. Her breath came in short, ragged gasps as she struggled to maintain her footing. Dapo's grip on her hand had loosened, and she could feel him beside her, though the world around them seemed to blur and warp in strange ways, making him appear as though he were miles away. Every step she took felt like it was pulling her deeper into the darkness, deeper into the Hollow that she could no longer escape.

Eleanor's eyes darted around, her mind racing. The trees were no longer familiar. They seemed twisted, their bark dark and rotting, their branches bending in unnatural angles, as though they were trying to touch her, to pull her into the earth itself. The air was thick with the stench of decay and the strange, acrid scent of something else—something ancient, dark, and suffocating. It filled her lungs, choking her from the inside out.

"Please," she whispered to herself, trying to steady her trembling hands. "Please, don't let it be true. Don't let this be real."

But the more she resisted, the more the Hollow pushed against her. It was inside her now, feeding off her doubts, her fear. She could feel it in her veins, crawling beneath her skin like an insidious infection. The whispers that had once been faint now screamed in her mind, drowning out everything else, pulling her deeper into its suffocating grip.

You can't escape. It's a part of you.

Eleanor squeezed her eyes shut, trying to block out the voice, but it was everywhere. It wasn't just in her head—it was in the air around her, in the trees, in the very ground she stood on. The Hollow was not an entity to be defeated. It wasn't a monster. It wasn't even a thing. It was an idea. A force. And it was inside her, just as the gatekeeper had said. It was part of her now. She could never outrun it.

"Eleanor..." Dapo's voice broke through the fog of her thoughts, pulling her back to the present. She turned to him, her eyes wide, but the sight of him made the darkness swirl even more violently. His face was pale, his expression strained, but he was still holding on to her. "We have to keep moving. We're almost there."

She didn't know what he meant by there, but the words seemed to push through her fear. He had always been the strong one, the one who could stand tall when everything else crumbled around them. She wanted to believe in him, to trust that he knew what he was doing, but the suffocating pressure of the

Hollow was almost too much to bear.

"Dapo..." Her voice trembled, barely above a whisper. "I can't do this anymore. I can't fight it."

His hand tightened on hers, pulling her toward him. His grip was warm and solid, a lifeline in the chaos that was threatening to swallow her whole. "Yes, you can. You have to, Eleanor. Don't let it win. Not now."

She shook her head, the words feeling like weights on her shoulders. "I'm not strong enough. I can't keep pretending I am. It's too much."

The Hollow was too much. The thought had been gnawing at her for days, weeks, maybe longer. She had been running from it—running from herself. But there was no running anymore. There was no place left to hide.

"I'm scared, Dapo," she whispered, her voice cracking. "What if it's already too late?"

For a long moment, he didn't speak. His gaze softened as he looked at her, his eyes filled with a mixture of sorrow and determination. Slowly, he stepped forward and placed a hand on her cheek, his touch gentle but firm.

"It's never too late," he said softly, his voice thick with emotion. "As long as we're still breathing, it's never too late."

The words should have comforted her. They should have given

her some kind of hope. But all she could hear was the Hollow, its voice clawing at her, pulling her deeper into the darkness. You're not strong enough. You belong to it.

Suddenly, the trees ahead of them seemed to part, revealing a clearing. Eleanor squinted into the darkness, but she couldn't make out what was beyond it. Something was waiting there— something that felt as though it had been waiting for them to reach this point. She took a hesitant step forward, but the ground beneath her feet seemed to shift, as though the earth itself was alive, shifting and breathing with the Hollow's presence.

"We have to go," Dapo urged, pulling her forward. "We don't have time."

But something in the back of Eleanor's mind stopped her. The clearing wasn't a place of safety. She could feel it. It was a place of reckoning. And she knew that, in order to move forward, she would have to confront whatever it was that had been chasing them. Whatever it was that had been stalking her since the moment she set foot in this cursed land.

She stopped in her tracks, pulling away from Dapo. "Wait."

His hand faltered, his brow furrowing in confusion. "What is it?"

"I can't go on like this," Eleanor said, her voice low and strained. "I can't keep pretending everything is okay. I can't keep pretending I'm okay."

Dapo's face softened, his eyes filled with concern. He reached out to touch her arm, his fingers brushing her skin gently. "Eleanor..."

"No," she cut him off, stepping back. "You don't understand. You don't know what it's like."

Her voice cracked, and the words rushed out before she could stop them.

"You think I'm strong. You think I can fight this. But I can't. I've been broken for so long, Dapo. This thing... the Hollow... it's inside me. It's always been inside me. And no matter how far I run, no matter how many times I try to escape, it's always there, lurking in the back of my mind, waiting to drag me down."

Tears welled up in her eyes, and for the first time, she let them fall. The dam had broken, and the flood of emotions poured out, washing over her in waves.

"I've been running from it for so long," she whispered. "And now... now I think it's too late to stop."

Dapo's expression faltered for a moment, his lips pressing together as though he didn't know what to say. He looked at her, his gaze soft, filled with sympathy, but also a deep, unsettling understanding. He didn't speak. He just reached for her, pulling her into his arms.

And in that moment, Eleanor let herself go. She let herself break. The weight of the Hollow, of everything she had been holding back, crashed over her like a tidal wave. She couldn't hold it in anymore. She couldn't keep pretending to be strong when every part of her was crumbling.

Dapo held her, his arms tight around her as she trembled in his embrace. He didn't say anything. He just let her cry, let her release the storm inside her. For a long time, they stood there in the clearing, the forest around them silent, the darkness pressing in, but Dapo's warmth kept the worst of it at bay.

Eventually, the storm inside her began to subside. The tears slowed, and her breathing steadied. She felt numb, drained, but for the first time in what felt like forever, she felt something resembling peace.

"You're not alone, Eleanor," Dapo whispered into her hair, his voice soft but firm. "We'll get through this. Together. You're stronger than you know."

Eleanor pulled back slightly, looking up at him, her eyes red from crying but filled with something else now. Hope. A fragile hope, but hope nonetheless. She wasn't sure if she could win. She wasn't sure if they could escape the Hollow, but she knew this: she didn't have to face it alone. And that, in itself, was a victory.

But as she looked into Dapo's eyes, a cold gust of wind swept through the clearing, rattling the trees. She shivered, instinctively pulling closer to him.

And then, from the darkness beyond the clearing, something

stirred. A shadow moved, large and heavy, its form taking shape in the dim light. Eleanor's breath caught in her throat as a figure emerged from the trees. A figure that was all too familiar.

It was the gatekeeper.

And this time, there would be no escape.

25

The Gatekeeper's Promise

The air in the clearing had turned frigid, the wind biting at Eleanor's skin as she stood frozen, her heart pounding in her chest. The figure that had stepped out from the shadows was unmistakable—tall, cloaked in shadows, with eyes that seemed to glow in the darkness. It was the gatekeeper. The one who had warned her. The one who had spoken of the Hollow, of its power, and of her place within it.

Eleanor felt the blood drain from her face. Her legs trembled, and for a moment, she thought she might collapse. But Dapo's arm was still around her, his grip firm, though she could feel his own tension radiating from him. He was ready. Ready for a fight. Ready for whatever this was.

The gatekeeper stood unmoving, a figure carved from the darkness itself. His face was obscured by the hood of his cloak, but Eleanor could see his eyes clearly—cold, ancient, and filled with a knowledge that seemed to pierce through her. The same eyes that had haunted her dreams, that had warned her that she was not free. Not yet. Not ever.

"You've come," the gatekeeper's voice echoed, deep and unsettling, like a whisper carried on the wind. It was the voice of something older than time itself, something that had seen the rise and fall of empires, the birth and death of stars.

Eleanor could hardly breathe. She wanted to speak, to ask him why he was here, why he had brought her to this place, but the words caught in her throat. What could she say to him? He had been right all along. The Hollow wasn't just a place. It was a part of her. A part of her that she could never escape.

Dapo stepped forward, his body tense, but his voice was clear as he spoke, his words sharp. "What do you want from us?"

The gatekeeper's gaze flickered toward Dapo, but he said nothing at first. He just stood there, watching them. The silence stretched on, heavy, suffocating, until Eleanor could no longer bear it. She stepped forward, her voice trembling but determined.

"What do you want with me?" she asked, her eyes never leaving the gatekeeper's. "Why did you bring me here? Why this place?"

The gatekeeper's lips twisted into something that could have been a smile, but there was no warmth in it—only the chill of a winter night. His voice, when it came, was quiet but filled with an unsettling certainty. "This is not a place you chose, Eleanor. This is a place you were always meant to come. The Hollow is within you. It always has been."

Eleanor recoiled, her heart skipping a beat. "No," she whispered, the word slipping out before she could stop it. "I didn't choose this. I didn't choose any of this."

The gatekeeper's eyes gleamed with an almost pitying look, as if he understood something she couldn't see. "No one chooses the Hollow, Eleanor. Not in the way you think. It chooses you. It claims you, just as it has claimed countless others before you."

A cold shiver ran down her spine. She felt Dapo's hand tighten on her arm, but she was already too lost in the gatekeeper's words. Her mind raced, trying to piece together what he was saying, but the truth eluded her, slipping through her fingers like water.

"What do you mean?" she asked, her voice barely above a whisper.

The gatekeeper didn't answer immediately. Instead, he stepped closer, his cloak swirling around him like a shadow. Every movement he made seemed deliberate, slow, almost as if he were savoring the moment. When he finally spoke, his words were heavy with meaning.

"The Hollow is a force that feeds on fear. On doubt. On the broken parts of the soul. It is not a place of torment, as you believe, but a mirror. A mirror that reflects the deepest parts of you, the parts you hide even from yourself. The Hollow reveals those parts and forces them to the surface."

Eleanor's stomach twisted. She had always felt something dark inside her, something broken, something incomplete. She had thought it was just her, her weakness, her flaw. But now she was beginning to understand—this was the Hollow. This was what had always been there, lurking beneath the surface.

"But why?" she whispered, her voice barely audible. "Why me?"

The gatekeeper's eyes seemed to burn into her soul as he spoke again, his voice both distant and intimate at the same time. "Because you are not whole, Eleanor. You never have been. You have always been incomplete. And the Hollow seeks that which is broken, that which can be remade."

Eleanor felt a surge of panic, her breath quickening as the weight of his words crashed over her. She wasn't whole. She wasn't complete. She had always known something was missing—something essential, something that made her who she was. But now she realized the truth: whatever the Hollow had touched, whatever it had broken inside her, could never be fixed. It had already claimed her. It was inside her. And no matter how hard she tried to run, she would never escape it.

"No," she gasped, shaking her head as tears welled in her eyes. "No, you're wrong. I'm not... I'm not like them."

"You are just like them," the gatekeeper said, his voice a soft, chilling murmur. "You have always been like them. You were born for this. Born to carry the Hollow within you."

Eleanor staggered back, her heart pounding in her chest. "I don't want this," she cried, her voice raw with the weight of her despair. "I didn't ask for this!"

The gatekeeper's eyes softened, almost as if he were looking at her with some semblance of compassion. "None of us ever ask for it," he said. "But we are all bound to it. The Hollow is not a curse—it is a calling. A destiny. And when the time comes, you will understand."

Dapo stepped in front of Eleanor, his body tense, his fists clenched at his sides. "What are you going to do to her?" he demanded, his voice filled with a mixture of fear and fury. "What do you want from us?"

The gatekeeper turned his gaze toward Dapo, his eyes narrowing. There was no malice in his expression, only the inevitability of something ancient and inescapable. "I want nothing from you," he said softly. "I do not control the Hollow. I only show the way. But Eleanor..." He paused, as if weighing his words carefully. "Eleanor has a choice to make."

Eleanor's heart stopped in her chest. "A choice?" she repeated, the word tasting bitter in her mouth. "What choice?"

The gatekeeper took another step forward, his gaze locked onto hers with an intensity that seemed to pierce her very soul. "The Hollow offers power, Eleanor. Power beyond your wildest imaginings. But it comes at a price. You will have to embrace it. You will have to become one with it. The question is—do you have the strength to do so?"

Eleanor's mind reeled, the weight of his words crashing over her like a storm. Power. The Hollow promised power. But what would it cost her? Her soul? Her humanity?

And what was the cost of refusing?

She looked at Dapo, her eyes searching his face for any sign of hope, for some answer. But he was as lost as she was. His eyes were filled with confusion, fear, and love—but no answers. They were in this together, but the path ahead was murky, obscured by the darkness that had begun to creep in around them.

The gatekeeper's voice broke the silence, low and foreboding. "Make your choice, Eleanor. You are not who you think you are. But you are what you choose to be."

Eleanor felt the cold rush of the wind as it swept through the clearing, carrying with it the weight of the gatekeeper's words. She was not who she thought she was. She was something else. Something broken, something incomplete. But now, the Hollow was offering her a choice. A choice between embracing it or destroying herself in the attempt to escape it.

Her mind spun, her heart racing in her chest as she stood at the edge of something dark and terrifying. The path ahead was a mystery, a blackened road that twisted in ways she could not predict. And in that moment, Eleanor knew—whatever choice she made now would shape her future forever.

And whatever choice she made... it would either break her—or make her whole.

26

The Choice of Darkness

Eleanor stood frozen, her chest heaving with every breath she struggled to take. The wind howled through the clearing, swirling around her in a frenzy, as though the very air was alive with anticipation. She couldn't feel her feet on the ground anymore, couldn't feel the cold or the damp earth beneath her boots. All she could feel was the weight of the gatekeeper's gaze, pressing on her from all directions, filling her with a terrifying sense of inevitability.

You are what you choose to be.

His words echoed in her mind, vibrating with a chilling resonance that seemed to pull at something deep inside her. The Hollow, the force that had haunted her since the moment she arrived, had always been a part of her. But now it was offering something she couldn't ignore—power, control, a way to bend the world to her will. And all she had to do was embrace it.

Eleanor's eyes flickered to Dapo, who was standing beside her, his jaw set in a grim line, his fists clenched. He was as terrified as she was, but he was trying to hide it—trying to keep his resolve strong for her. He had always been the one who kept her grounded, the one who had shown her what love and loyalty could look like. But now, standing before the gatekeeper, before the Hollow itself, Eleanor could feel the fragility of that bond. The love she had for Dapo, the love they had built together, was suddenly dwarfed by the magnitude of the choice she was facing.

The gatekeeper's voice broke through her thoughts, his words smooth as silk, but laced with an unspoken promise. "You have felt it, haven't you, Eleanor? The power that stirs inside you. The power that is part of you. The Hollow is not just a place. It is a force, a part of your very soul. You cannot escape it. You were born for this moment."

Eleanor's heart raced as she looked at the gatekeeper, unable to tear her gaze away from the darkness in his eyes. The choice he was offering wasn't one she had asked for—it wasn't one she wanted. But the truth was undeniable. She could feel the Hollow inside her, gnawing at her from the inside out, urging her to let go, to embrace it. It was like a hunger, a gnawing desire that would never be satisfied unless she gave in.

Her hand tightened around Dapo's, her fingers cold and clammy, as though the very act of touching him could ground her in reality. But nothing felt real anymore. Not the trees that bent in unnatural ways. Not the wind that whispered secrets she couldn't understand. And certainly not the gatekeeper, whose very presence seemed to warp the fabric of the world around her.

Dapo's voice was low, barely a whisper, but it cut through the air with a quiet urgency. "Eleanor... please. Don't listen to him. This isn't you. This... this isn't who you are."

His words should have been comforting. They should have been the anchor she needed to fight the darkness, to hold onto the love that had always guided her. But they felt hollow now. How could she hold on to something when she wasn't even sure who she was anymore?

The gatekeeper chuckled softly, the sound like the rustling of dry leaves in a storm. "You see, Dapo, your words cannot reach her. Not anymore. She is beyond your reach, beyond anyone's reach now. The Hollow has claimed her, just as it claims all those who are meant for it."

Eleanor shook her head, trying to block out the gatekeeper's voice, but his words were like tendrils of darkness, wrapping around her mind, dragging her deeper into the void. She wanted to scream, to break free, but something inside her—a part of her she couldn't name—wanted to listen. Wanted to give in. The hunger inside her was growing stronger, more insistent.

"You don't have to do this, Eleanor," Dapo said, his voice thick with emotion. "You don't have to let it win. I don't care what the gatekeeper says. I don't care what he promises. You are stronger than this. You are stronger than it."

His words felt like a lifeline thrown into a sea of darkness, but the current was too strong. The pull of the Hollow was too great.

"I'm scared, Dapo," Eleanor whispered, her voice trembling. "I'm scared of what I'll become if I refuse it. I'm scared of what's inside me. What if... what if I'm already lost?"

Dapo's eyes softened, and he stepped closer to her, his hand resting on her shoulder, grounding her. "You're not lost, Eleanor. You're here. With me. You're not broken. You're not a thing to be fixed by the Hollow. You're you. And that's all that matters."

But the gatekeeper's laughter sliced through the air, cruel and hollow. "You—a thing to be fixed? How quaint. You can't see it, can you? How much of yourself you've already given to the Hollow. The fragments you've abandoned. The pieces you've lost."

Eleanor winced as the gatekeeper's words sank deep into her soul, carving a wound she couldn't heal. It was true. She had been running from the truth for so long, hiding pieces of herself she didn't want to face. Her fear, her insecurities, her brokenness—they had always been there, lurking beneath the surface, waiting for the right moment to reveal themselves. And now, in the presence of the Hollow, they were impossible to ignore.

Dapo reached for her again, his fingers gentle against her skin. "Please, Eleanor. Don't listen to him. I know you. I know what you are capable of. You're not broken. You're not a shadow of yourself. You're a whole person, and I believe in you. Don't let him tell you otherwise."

Eleanor's chest tightened, and for a moment, it felt like the weight of the world was pressing in on her. Her eyes darted between Dapo and the gatekeeper, the two forces pulling at her, one filled with love, the other with a dark promise of power. Her thoughts swirled, her mind a blur of conflicting emotions and desires. Could she walk away from the Hollow? Could she walk away from the thing that had become a part of her, that had always been a part of her?

Is it too late?

The question lingered in her mind, unanswered, as she faced the decision that would determine her fate.

The gatekeeper took a slow, deliberate step forward, his shadow stretching across the clearing like a dark omen. "The Hollow will never leave you, Eleanor. It is part of you. You cannot escape it. But you can embrace it. You can become one with it. You can wield its power, control it, and shape the world around you as you see fit."

Eleanor felt the weight of those words sink into her bones. Power. Control. They were intoxicating promises. Promises that offered her a way out, a way to finally feel whole, finally feel in command of her own destiny.

But at what cost?

Dapo's voice broke through her thoughts again, steady and

unwavering. "Eleanor, listen to me. The power the gatekeeper speaks of—it's not freedom. It's a prison. You'd be giving up your soul, your humanity, for a false promise. You are more than the Hollow. You are more than its darkness. You are you. You are whole. Don't let it take that from you."

The battle raged inside Eleanor, the words of Dapo and the gatekeeper echoing in her mind like the clash of two opposing forces. She could feel the Hollow's hunger gnawing at her, its promise of power, its lure of control. But she also felt Dapo's warmth, his presence, grounding her. She felt the love that had always anchored her, the love that had kept her going even when everything else felt like it was falling apart.

She closed her eyes, taking a deep breath, as the weight of her choice pressed down on her. She had to decide. She had to choose, not just for herself, but for the future, for Dapo, for everything she had fought to protect.

The Hollow offered power, but Dapo offered love. The gatekeeper offered control, but Dapo offered freedom.

Eleanor opened her eyes, her heart steady now, her resolve firm. She took a step forward, moving away from the gatekeeper, away from the darkness that had tried to claim her.

"I choose freedom," she said, her voice unwavering.

The gatekeeper's eyes flared with a sudden fury, but Eleanor didn't flinch. She had made her choice.

And no matter what the cost, she would not let the Hollow take her soul.

27

The Breaking Point

The moment Eleanor spoke those words, she felt the ground beneath her feet tremble. It wasn't a physical shaking, but something deeper—a shift in the air, a rending of the fabric of reality itself. She could feel it, the Hollow, recoiling as though it had been struck, its hunger momentarily stilled. But the force of it was far from gone. It was only waiting. Watching.

The gatekeeper's eyes darkened as he took a step toward her, his figure casting a shadow that stretched unnaturally long across the clearing. His smile, when it came, was cold and full of disdain. It was the smile of someone who knew victory was inevitable, someone who had already seen the end of the story play out in their mind.

"You choose freedom?" His voice was a low, mocking whisper, carried on the wind like a death sentence. "Foolish girl. You are nothing but a puppet. You cannot outrun what is inside you. You cannot escape what was always meant to be."

Eleanor's heart pounded in her chest, and for a moment, she was certain the Hollow would consume her, just as the gatekeeper had promised. But she could hear Dapo's voice in her mind, steady, unwavering, reminding her of who she was. You are not broken. You are whole. You are you.

It was enough to steel her resolve. She turned to him, her eyes locking with his, her grip tightening on his hand. She didn't need words—he understood. They were in this together, no matter what the Hollow tried to do. No matter what it threatened to take from them.

The gatekeeper's expression faltered, just for a moment, as if he had expected her to fall. But when Eleanor didn't waver, when she stood her ground, his eyes narrowed. A shift occurred, something subtle yet undeniable in the air. The world around them seemed to dim, as if the Hollow itself was drawing its breath in preparation for something terrible.

"You think you are strong enough?" the gatekeeper sneered, his voice thick with venom. "You think you can deny the power of the Hollow? You are nothing but a speck in the dark. A fleeting moment, nothing more. And in the end, the Hollow will consume you. It will break you, just as it has broken countless others before you."

The words stung, but Eleanor didn't flinch. Instead, she felt a surge of something unfamiliar deep inside her, something that wasn't the Hollow, but something stronger. Something human. Something that had always been there, buried beneath the weight of the darkness.

Dapo stepped closer to her, his hand resting on her shoulder, grounding her, as he had always done. "We're not afraid of you," he said, his voice steady, though there was a fire in his eyes that Eleanor had never seen before. "We won't let you win."

The gatekeeper laughed, a sound that echoed through the clearing like the sound of bones breaking. It was a laugh that made Eleanor's skin crawl, a laugh that told her everything she needed to know: this battle was far from over.

"You don't understand, do you?" the gatekeeper hissed. "You are already lost. The Hollow is within you. It has always been within you. It is not something you can fight. You cannot run from it. It is you."

The words hit Eleanor like a blow to the chest. The Hollow. The thing she had been running from all her life. The thing she had feared, the thing that had haunted her dreams, the thing that had always been just beneath the surface of her skin. Was it true? Was she really nothing but the Hollow's vessel, its puppet?

"No," Eleanor whispered, shaking her head. "I won't believe it. I am more than this. I am not what you say I am."

But even as she said it, she felt a creeping doubt settle in her mind. The gatekeeper's words were like poison, seeping into her thoughts, twisting them, forcing her to question everything she had ever known. Could she really fight this thing inside her? Was there a way to overcome it without losing herself? Or was the Hollow truly part of her, a part of her that could never be cast aside?

The wind howled again, a violent gust that pushed her back, forcing her to stumble. The clearing seemed to grow darker, the edges of the world blurring, as if the very fabric of reality was beginning to tear apart. Eleanor's vision wavered, the shadows creeping closer, swallowing the light. She could feel it now, the Hollow inside her, pulsing like a living thing, beating in time with her own heart. The hunger was there, gnawing at her, pulling at her from the inside.

It was too much. The pressure was overwhelming. She could feel herself slipping, could feel her thoughts being pulled in different directions, all of them dark, all of them laced with fear.

"I can't do this," she gasped, clutching her head, her hands trembling as she tried to hold herself together. "I can't fight it. It's too much. I'm not strong enough."

Dapo's voice cut through the chaos, sharp and clear. "Yes, you are, Eleanor. You've always been stronger than you think. The Hollow can't break you. Not if you don't let it."

His words were a lifeline, a tether that kept her from falling into the abyss. Eleanor clung to them, clung to him, as the world around her began to collapse. The shadows seemed to stretch, dark tendrils reaching toward her, pulling at her mind, urging her to surrender. The gatekeeper's face twisted in a grin of triumph as he saw the fear in her eyes.

"You see?" he said, his voice low and insidious. "It is already too late. The darkness is in you. You cannot fight it. You are its servant, its pawn. You will always be."

Eleanor's chest tightened as the truth of his words clawed at her. She had always been broken, always been lost. The Hollow wasn't something that had come to her. It was inside her. It was part of her. She could feel it, hear it, its whispers growing louder, more insistent. It was drowning her, suffocating her. Her mind screamed for release, for a way out.

But then Dapo's hand found hers again, warm and strong. "You are not your darkness, Eleanor," he said, his voice filled with an intensity that made her heart beat faster. "You are the light. You are more than this. You are you. And I will never leave you, not even in the darkest moments."

Eleanor's breath caught in her throat as his words sank in. She wasn't broken. She wasn't lost. She wasn't the Hollow. She was Eleanor. And no matter how much the gatekeeper tried to tear her apart, she could fight it. She would fight it.

The gatekeeper's face darkened, his eyes narrowing with fury as he saw the shift in her. "You think you can fight me?" he spat. "You think you can resist what is inevitable? You are nothing."

Eleanor straightened, lifting her chin as she met his gaze. She could feel the darkness within her, its cold fingers curling around her heart, but she wasn't afraid anymore. Not of the gatekeeper. Not of the Hollow. She had her own power, her own strength, and it was far more than the Hollow could ever offer her.

"No," she said, her voice steady, her eyes never leaving the gatekeeper's. "I'm not nothing. I'm Eleanor. And I will not let you control me."

The clearing seemed to hold its breath. The wind died down, and for a moment, the world was silent, as if the entire universe were waiting for what would come next. The gatekeeper's eyes flickered, and Eleanor could see the shift in him, the first hint of uncertainty. It was small, barely perceptible, but it was there.

And in that moment, she knew. She knew that she had won. She had chosen her own path, her own destiny. She wasn't the Hollow's servant, and she never would be.

The gatekeeper's form began to flicker, the shadows that had once enveloped him beginning to unravel, as though his very essence was starting to fade. His face twisted into a snarl, but there was nothing left of the certainty he had once carried. "This isn't over, Eleanor," he hissed, his voice growing fainter, weaker. "The Hollow will find you again. It will always find you."

Eleanor stepped forward, her heart steady, her voice calm but filled with a quiet power. "Maybe. But I'll be ready."

And with that, the gatekeeper's form disintegrated into nothingness, swallowed by the darkness that had once bound him. The shadows receded, and the clearing began to return to its natural state, the winds calming, the air clearing. Eleanor and Dapo were alone, standing in the silence, the weight of the battle still hanging heavy between them.

Dapo's hand found hers once more, and this time, it was a reminder. A reminder of who they were. Of who they would always be. Together.

Eleanor smiled, a small, knowing smile. The Hollow may have been inside her, but it didn't own her. She had made her choice, and she would never let it break her.

Not now. Not ever.

28

Into the Abyss

The clearing was eerily quiet now, the sounds of the battle with the gatekeeper fading into the background like a distant memory. Eleanor stood at its center, her breath steady but her heart racing. The air, once thick with the presence of the Hollow, now felt almost suffocating in its silence. She could feel the lingering shadows of the past, the taste of the gatekeeper's words still fresh on her tongue.

But there was no time to rest, no time to savor the small victory. The Hollow was not done with her. It never would be.

Dapo's hand was still gripping hers, strong and unwavering, as though he, too, could sense the shift in the air—the looming presence of something greater, something far darker. The world around them seemed to pulse with an unseen energy, the trees whispering in the wind as though sharing secrets she could not understand.

"Are you alright?" Dapo's voice broke through the stillness, his concern obvious in the way his eyes searched her face. "You're not... you're not fading again, are you?"

Eleanor shook her head quickly, brushing off his concern

with a faint smile. "No. I'm fine." The words came out sharper than she intended, but she couldn't help it. She had to convince herself. *I am fine.*

But the truth was, she wasn't. The Hollow still lingered inside her like a poison, threatening to resurface at any moment. She could feel its pulse, faint but undeniable, like the beat of her own heart—demanding, relentless, whispering promises of power and freedom. She was *this close* to giving in. The temptation was a heavy weight on her chest, a heavy weight in her thoughts.

Dapo squeezed her hand tighter, pulling her from her spiraling thoughts. "Eleanor, listen to me," he said, his voice low but firm. "You don't have to face this alone. Whatever happens next, I'm with you. Always."

She wanted to believe him, wanted to let his words comfort her, but there was a truth she couldn't deny. The Hollow was inside her. And in the end, it would take everything. It always did.

"What if it's too much this time, Dapo?" Her voice trembled, though she hated the vulnerability in it. "What if I can't control it anymore? What if I become... like him?"

Dapo's expression softened, his fingers brushing her cheek gently. "You're not him. You'll never be him, Eleanor. You are stronger than you think. You are *you*. You've always been."

But her mind was elsewhere, her thoughts whirling like a storm. They were both standing on the edge of something vast, something dangerous, and no amount of reassurance could change the simple fact: the Hollow had always been part of her, and that bond was not easily broken.

A sudden chill swept through the clearing, causing Eleanor to shiver involuntarily. The shadows shifted around them, stretching and writhing, as if the darkness itself was alive, watching, waiting. Eleanor's heart skipped a beat. The Hollow wasn't gone. It was just biding its time.

From the corner of her eye, she saw it. The trees, once still and unmoving, were bending, twisting unnaturally, as if something was pushing them to their breaking point. The ground beneath their feet began to tremble again, a low rumble that sent a ripple of dread through her body. The clearing wasn't just quiet—it was *waiting*. The air was thick with a sense of impending doom, and she couldn't ignore it.

Dapo's face was hardening, his brow furrowing with concern as he followed her gaze. "It's happening again," he said, his voice strained. "Eleanor, we need to get out of here. Now."

But Eleanor couldn't move. Her body was frozen in place, every muscle locked in place as she stared into the heart of the forest. Something was coming. Something far worse than the gatekeeper.

A deep, guttural growl echoed through the trees, a sound that seemed to rattle the very bones of the earth. Eleanor's pulse quickened. She had heard that sound before—back when she had first entered the Hollow, back when she had felt the first tendrils of darkness creeping into her soul.

The ground shook harder now, sending ripples of energy through the air. The trees swayed violently, their branches scraping against one another like the claws of some great beast. The clearing was being pulled apart. The very world itself was beginning to fracture.

"What is that?" Dapo asked, his voice tight with fear.

Eleanor could barely answer. The answer was already clear. It was the Hollow, alive and angry, ready to devour everything in its path. And it was coming for them.

A figure emerged from the darkness at the edge of the

clearing, its silhouette tall and menacing. It moved with a fluid, almost unnatural grace, as though the very air parted before it. Eleanor's heart skipped as recognition struck her like a thunderclap.

The figure was *him*. The gatekeeper. But this time, there was no mocking smile on his face. There was no arrogance, no confidence. This time, he was different. The air around him crackled with power, with an energy that made the hairs on the back of Eleanor's neck stand on end.

"No," she whispered. "It can't be."

But there was no denying it. The figure standing before them was the gatekeeper. But now he was more than just a man. He was a manifestation of the Hollow itself. His body was shifting, twisting, as though it were made of smoke and shadows. His form was no longer human. It was monstrous.

His eyes glowed with an otherworldly light, bright and cold, and as they locked onto Eleanor, she felt the weight of his gaze press down on her like an unbearable weight. The darkness within her stirred, thrumming with recognition. The Hollow was calling her. It was pulling her in, like a moth to a flame.

The gatekeeper's voice slithered through the air, cold and menacing. "You cannot hide from it, Eleanor. It is here. And you... you are mine."

Eleanor's breath hitched. The darkness inside her stirred again, its hunger growing, its whispers louder, more demanding. She could feel it, tugging at her, calling her to come closer. To surrender.

But Dapo's hand in hers was a lifeline. His grip was tight, his fingers digging into her skin, as if he, too, could sense the power of the Hollow creeping into the world around them.

"We won't let it take you," he said, his voice firm, though his own fear was evident. "We're stronger than this."

But the gatekeeper only laughed, the sound echoing through the trees like the crack of thunder. "You cannot stop what has already begun," he sneered. "The Hollow is everywhere. It is within you, Eleanor. It is within all of us. There is no escaping it."

Eleanor's chest tightened. She could feel the weight of his words. The Hollow had always been a part of her. She could feel it now, its power pulsing inside her, demanding her surrender. The more she resisted, the stronger it became, until it felt like her mind was being ripped apart by the force of it.

"No," she said again, more fiercely this time. "I am not a part of you. I am not yours."

The gatekeeper's eyes flashed with fury, and with a sudden, terrifying movement, he lunged at them, his form shifting into something even darker, more monstrous, as he reached for Eleanor. The very air seemed to grow colder as he neared, his hand crackling with energy that hummed through the ground beneath their feet.

Dapo reacted instantly, pulling Eleanor backward, his arm shielding her as he stepped between her and the gatekeeper. "Stay behind me," he ordered, his voice hard but filled with determination.

Eleanor's heart was racing, the Hollow's whispers louder now, urging her to give in, to let it take control. She felt the pull, the hunger inside her, the promise of power. But she also felt something else—something stronger. Dapo's unwavering presence. His love. His belief in her.

And in that moment, Eleanor realized something. She wasn't just resisting the Hollow. She wasn't just fighting the darkness. She was fighting for *her*—for the person she had always been, for the person she was meant to be.

The ground beneath them cracked open with a deafening roar, and the world seemed to bend as the gatekeeper's form loomed closer, his hand reaching for Eleanor's throat.

But Eleanor wasn't afraid anymore. Not of him. Not of the Hollow.

She stepped forward, pulling Dapo's hand with her, and faced the gatekeeper head-on, her eyes burning with the determination that had always been her greatest strength.

"I will not let you break me," she said, her voice clear and unyielding.

The gatekeeper stopped in his tracks, his eyes narrowing with confusion. For the first time, there was uncertainty in his gaze. Eleanor felt the power inside her surge, the darkness inside her no longer controlling her, but *tamed* by her will.

"This ends now," she said, her voice ringing out with authority, as if the very words could shatter the world around them.

And as she spoke, the darkness began to recede. Slowly, but surely, the gatekeeper's form began to flicker and fade, the Hollow's power that had once seemed so vast now retreating in the face of her defiance.

Eleanor had made her choice.

29

The Final Hour

The world seemed to hold its breath as the gatekeeper's form began to dissipate before Eleanor's eyes. His figure, once towering and monstrous, flickered like a dying flame, the shadows around him unraveling in every direction. Eleanor could feel the power she had harnessed, the strength that surged from deep within her, but she also felt the echo of the Hollow's presence still clinging to her, reluctant to let go.

Dapo's grip tightened around her hand, his fingers steady but with an underlying tremor that she could feel even through the thick walls of her own growing resolve. He hadn't let go of her. He hadn't backed down. And that, more than anything, was what kept her grounded as the world around them unraveled.

The clearing was now bathed in an unnatural stillness, the air heavy with the scent of burned earth and damp leaves. The ground beneath their feet was cracking, the fissures spreading like veins of darkness, threatening to swallow them whole. But Eleanor couldn't focus on that. She couldn't focus on anything but the fading figure of the gatekeeper, who was now little more than a wisp of smoke, his twisted form folding into the shadows, vanishing into the abyss from which it came.

And then, as the gatekeeper's presence completely dissolved into the darkness, there was silence. Utter, suffocating silence.

Eleanor felt it first—like the emptiness of the space around them had sucked every last breath from her lungs. Dapo's hand was still gripping hers, but now it was as if the world had come to a complete standstill. Her heartbeat echoed in her ears, and the silence was so profound that it felt unnatural. She couldn't remember the last time she'd heard nothing at all.

The Hollow's whispers, which had once been a constant hum at the edges of her mind, were gone. The pressure on her chest, the weight of the darkness that had once threatened to crush her, seemed to lift. But the victory felt hollow. It wasn't over. It couldn't be.

"Eleanor," Dapo's voice broke through the stillness, his tone low but strained, as if he, too, could feel the tremors beneath the surface. "It's not done yet. I can feel it."

Her eyes, wide and alert, scanned the clearing, the trees, the sky above them. She could sense it, too—the unsettling stillness that wasn't quite peace. It was something far worse, far more dangerous. A calm before the storm. The Hollow hadn't truly disappeared. It had only retreated... for now.

A sudden gust of wind swept through the trees, bending them

low as if to warn them of the impending threat. The rustling of leaves sounded almost like whispers, like the Hollow's voice, but deeper, darker. More ancient. The air grew cold, and Eleanor felt the familiar chill that came with the darkness creeping back into her soul.

"Dapo..." Her voice was barely a whisper, the words caught in her throat as the very earth beneath them seemed to hum with unnatural energy. She could feel the ground shifting, the pull of the abyss growing stronger, threatening to drag them both into the very heart of the Hollow.

Dapo stepped closer to her, his hand still firm around hers. "Stay close. We're not safe here."

It wasn't just the Hollow that was dangerous. It was everything—everything she had uncovered in the last few days, the truths she had learned, the promises that had been whispered into her ears, the choices she had made. They were all leading to this moment, to the final confrontation. The Hollow had not been the only threat. The gatekeeper, with all his power, had only been a servant of something far older, far more dangerous. The Hollow had a master, and Eleanor was about to face it.

"I—I can't do this, Dapo," she confessed, her voice breaking as she felt the pressure rising again, the pull of darkness growing stronger. "I can't control it. I don't think I can fight it any longer."

Dapo's expression softened, but his grip on her hand remained firm. "You can do this, Eleanor. You've always been able to. You've fought it this far. And I'll be with you—every step of the way."

His words, though full of love and reassurance, did nothing to quiet the growing storm inside her. She could feel the Hollow's presence once again—like an old friend that had returned after a long absence, only this time, its whispers were louder, sharper, its hunger more insistent. The shadows stretched toward her, wrapping around her like cold fingers, each one a reminder of her weakness, each one a promise of what it could take if she let it.

"Dapo," Eleanor said again, this time her voice shaking with something far deeper than fear. "What if I become the thing I'm trying to stop? What if I can't control it any longer?"

He didn't answer immediately. Instead, he stepped closer, closing the space between them. His breath was warm against her skin, his presence a comfort in a world that seemed to be collapsing around them.

"You won't become what you fear, Eleanor," he said, his voice steady but filled with a quiet urgency. "You're stronger than this. The Hollow can't define you. It can't own you. You're more than the darkness inside you. You're more than all of this."

The words, though comforting, felt like fragile threads in the face of the storm that was now swelling in her chest. She could feel the power of the Hollow growing stronger, could feel the storm rising to meet her. The shadows at the edges of her vision grew thicker, swirling like a vortex, ready to pull her under. The power she had felt before—the power that had driven her—was now a living, breathing thing inside her, tugging at her with promises of control, of power, of freedom from everything that had held her back.

But freedom wasn't what the Hollow wanted. It wasn't freedom at all. The Hollow wanted her soul. It wanted her heart.

"I'm scared, Dapo," she whispered, unable to stop herself, her voice a mix of sorrow and terror. "I don't want to become the thing I hate."

Dapo said nothing for a long moment, his eyes locked on hers. And then, in a voice so low it was almost lost in the wind, he said, "We'll fight it together."

His words broke something inside her—some barrier that had held her back for so long. And for the first time in what felt like forever, Eleanor made a choice. A choice to not let the Hollow take her. To not let it win. To not give in to the darkness that had been clawing at her from the inside out.

The clearing, which had been silent moments before, seemed to thrum with energy as the ground shifted beneath them. The sky above them darkened, the once-soft clouds now swirling in a violent storm, as though the heavens themselves were reacting to the chaos that was unfolding on earth. The air grew heavy with the sense that something terrible was coming.

Without warning, the earth beneath their feet split open, the ground trembling violently as if the very foundations of the world were crumbling. A surge of dark energy erupted from the fissure, a maelstrom of black shadows that seemed to devour the light, twisting and spiraling upward. Eleanor felt it immediately—the weight of the Hollow's power, growing stronger, more concentrated with each passing second.

A figure emerged from the depths of the darkness, its shape twisted and impossible to comprehend. It was both everywhere and nowhere, a being that seemed to exist between realms, neither fully tangible nor fully ethereal. But one thing was clear: it was the source of the Hollow. It was the master—the heart of the darkness that had been waiting all this time.

The world held its breath, as if the universe itself were waiting for her next move.

And in that moment, Eleanor knew. There would be no escape. No simple resolution. The fight for her soul, for her future, for everything she had ever cared about, was about to begin.

But this time, she wasn't alone.

Dapo stood beside her. And together, they would face the darkness.

It was the final hour.

30

The Heart of the Hollow

The ground trembled beneath Eleanor's feet, a deep, guttural rumble that shook her to the core. Her heart raced in her chest, her breath coming in quick, shallow gasps. The air around them crackled with dark energy, the atmosphere thick with a malevolent presence that filled every corner of the clearing. The figure that had risen from the depths of the Hollow was now fully formed—its shadow stretching across the land like a living, breathing thing. The storm overhead mirrored the chaos below, its swirling clouds forming a perfect vortex above them, the heavens seemingly conspiring with the forces of darkness.

Eleanor could feel the weight of it. The suffocating power of the Hollow, the ancient, insatiable hunger that had been pulling at her from within. But there was something else, too. A flicker of defiance, a spark of resistance that burned in her chest. The storm within her mirrored the storm above—turbulent, uncontrollable, but capable of breaking free.

Dapo's hand was still tightly wrapped around hers, his fingers pressing into her skin with a quiet urgency. He was here. He was with her. And as the darkness roiled around them, he was the only thing that kept her tethered to the world she had fought so hard to protect.

The figure in front of them—no longer a man, but an embodiment of pure darkness—towered like an ancient titan. It was massive, its form an ever-shifting mass of shadows, a swirling vortex of lightless energy. It was both there and not there, as if it existed in a realm beyond their comprehension. But its eyes… those eyes glowed, cold and unfeeling, like two burning coals in a void of nothingness. And they were fixed on Eleanor.

She could feel its gaze like a physical weight, crushing her beneath its unrelenting stare. It knew her. It had always known her. And now, it was ready to claim her.

Eleanor's breath caught in her throat. Her mind swirled with the Hollow's whispers, its promises of power and freedom, its dark lullaby that beckoned her to surrender, to join it. She could feel its fingers tightening around her soul, threatening to rip her apart. The darkness inside her was this close to overwhelming her, to swallowing her whole.

"Eleanor," Dapo's voice was low, strained, as if he, too, could feel the pressure building. "You have to fight it. You are not it. You are not them. You're stronger than this."

Eleanor's eyes closed for a moment, and she felt the truth of his words deep in her bones. She was stronger. She had always been stronger than the Hollow, stronger than the darkness inside her. But that didn't mean it was easy. It didn't mean it would let go. The Hollow was not just a force of nature; it was a part of her. And every fiber of her being screamed at her to give in. To let go.

But she couldn't. Not now. Not when so much was at stake.

Her grip tightened around Dapo's hand, and she looked up at him, meeting his eyes for the first time since the darkness had descended. There was fear in his gaze, but there was something else too. Hope. Belief. In her.

"We can't stop this alone," she said, her voice a mixture of desperation and resolve. "But together, maybe... maybe we can."

Dapo nodded, his lips pressing into a thin line, his jaw set. "Together," he repeated, and for the first time, Eleanor could hear the certainty in his voice. "We fight together."

She nodded back, the words filling her with strength she didn't know she had. The Hollow was powerful, but it was not invincible. The figure in front of them—the master of the Hollow—was its true source. And that was the key. If they could destroy it, if they could sever the heart of the darkness, they could end this. Once and for all.

The figure before them—the thing that was no longer human, that was no longer a thing of flesh—moved, its form undulating like a black tide, as though it were a living, breathing storm. The ground cracked beneath its feet, the very air trembling in its presence.

"You cannot fight what is already inside you, Eleanor," the Hollow's voice boomed, deep and resonant, like the echo of ancient thunder. "You were born to serve me. You will never escape me."

Eleanor's pulse quickened as the voice seemed to reverberate in her mind. It was the voice of the darkness, the voice of the Hollow that had been with her since the beginning. She could feel it now, clawing at her mind, pulling at her thoughts, threatening to drown her in its cold embrace.

But she would not fall.

"I am not yours," Eleanor said, her voice unwavering, even as the darkness swirled around her, suffocating her with its power. "I will never be yours."

The Hollow's laughter rang through the clearing, low and mocking, like the sound of a predator toying with its prey. "You are already mine, Eleanor. You always have been."

And in that moment, Eleanor understood. The Hollow had never been just a force of darkness. It was not some entity that existed outside of her, some foreign power that had invaded her life. No. The Hollow had always been a part of her. It had always existed in the space between the light and the dark, between who she was and who she feared she might become. It was the shadow in the corner of her mind, the doubt, the fear, the part of her that had always wanted to give in.

But she would not let it win.

She closed her eyes, and in that moment, she let the darkness inside her rage. She let it rise, let it twist and coil, but this time, she did not fear it. She embraced it. She could feel the Hollow's power coursing through her, but she did not succumb. She took it and made it her own, bending it to her will.

The ground beneath them rumbled again, and the darkness around them thickened, but Eleanor stood tall, her chest rising with the newfound strength that surged through her. She could feel the power of the Hollow, yes, but now, it was her power. And she would not let it consume her. Not again.

The figure in front of them seemed to recoil, as though the very essence of Eleanor's defiance had shaken it. Its form twisted, the darkness around it warping like a stormcloud caught in the winds of an unseen force. The Hollow's eyes narrowed, glowing brighter as it surged forward, its voice now a hiss, an angry snarl.

"You will be mine," it growled, and the earth beneath them cracked wide open, sending a wave of energy that knocked Eleanor and Dapo to their knees.

But Dapo did not let go of her hand. He pulled her back up, his strength unwavering, his eyes locked on hers. "We fight together, Eleanor. You're not alone."

And in that moment, Eleanor felt it. The Hollow might have been inside her, but it was not in control. She was the one in control. She had always been the one in control.

With a surge of power, Eleanor raised her free hand, calling upon the darkness inside her, but this time, she did not let it consume her. She used it. Used it as a weapon, a force of nature that she commanded. The shadows around her writhed and twisted, but instead of trying to escape, she shaped them, molded them into something new, something powerful. The dark energy became a shield, a barrier between her and the Hollow, and the figure in front of her recoiled, its form shrinking in fear.

Eleanor's heart raced, but her mind was clear. The Hollow might have been a part of her, but it was not who she was. It did not define her. The truth was simple: Eleanor was not a puppet of the darkness. She was its master.

With a roar, she unleashed the power she had forged, sending a blast of dark energy toward the Hollow's heart. The figure screamed, a sound that echoed like a thousand voices wailing in pain, as the very fabric of its form began to unravel. The shadows that had once defined it were now consumed by her light, by the force of her defiance. The storm overhead seemed to shudder as the Hollow's power broke apart, the darkness scattering like ash in the wind.

Eleanor collapsed to her knees, exhausted, but victorious. The ground around them was still, and for the first time in what felt like forever, she felt at peace. The storm in her chest had quieted, the Hollow's whispers fading into nothingness.

Dapo knelt beside her, his hand on her shoulder, his eyes filled with relief. "You did it, Eleanor. You did it."

And as the world around them began to heal, as the darkness receded, Eleanor allowed herself a single, quiet breath of triumph.

It was over.

But she knew—deep down, in the deepest parts of her soul—that the battle for the heart of the Hollow was never truly over. It would always be a part of her. But she was stronger now. And for the first time, Eleanor understood what it meant to be free.

The storm had passed. The Hollow was no more.

31

Into the Light

The first thing Eleanor noticed was the silence. The deep, all-encompassing quiet that followed the storm was absolute. No wind rustled the leaves. No birds dared to sing. The air was thick, still, as though the world itself was holding its breath. Even the earth, which had trembled and cracked beneath the force of the Hollow's power, seemed to have stilled, as though it, too, were waiting.

Dapo's hand was still pressed firmly against her shoulder, and the warmth of his touch grounded her in the aftermath of what had just transpired. She had fought the Hollow and won. She had faced the darkness inside her and emerged victorious. The figure that had haunted her for so long—an ancient being born of shadow and fear—was gone. But even as she stood there, breathing in the suffocating stillness, something inside her told her that this victory was fragile, like a delicate glass poised on the edge of a precipice.

She lifted her head slowly, scanning the clearing. The place where the Hollow's master had stood was now empty—empty, but not quite still. The very earth felt wrong, as though the removal of such a dark force had left a hollow echo in its wake, an emptiness that tugged at her heart. The air was heavy with the scent of burnt wood and damp earth, the remnants of the battle that had ravaged this place. And the darkness? The one she had embraced, the one that had fought her at every turn—its remnants lingered in her chest, like a shadow that refused to fade, no matter how much light she tried to shine upon it.

Eleanor closed her eyes for a moment, feeling the pulse of her own heartbeat, trying to steady the tremors in her hands. She had done it. She had fought back the Hollow, but in doing so, she had also faced the darkest parts of herself—the parts that had nearly consumed her. The parts that were her.

"You're not alone," Dapo's voice broke through her thoughts, soft and steady. His words had always been a balm, soothing the raw edges of her fear, but today, his voice carried the weight of their shared struggle. "It's over now. The Hollow's gone."

Eleanor nodded, though part of her wasn't sure if the Hollow was truly gone. She could still feel its presence deep inside her, the remnants of the darkness swirling at the edges of her consciousness, beckoning her to return. To give in.

"I don't know, Dapo," she whispered, her voice barely audible above the oppressive silence. "I can still feel it. It's still in me. The Hollow didn't just leave. It's... part of me."

Dapo's hand tightened around hers, pulling her toward him

gently. His eyes met hers, and there was a deep, quiet understanding in them. He knew. He knew what it was like to battle with an unseen enemy, to fight with the ghosts of one's own mind. He, too, had carried darkness inside him, in his own way. But there was something else in his gaze—something that spoke of strength and trust, of belief.

"You're stronger than it," he said, his voice low but unshakable. "You've always been. The Hollow may have been inside you, but it's not who you are. You know that now, Eleanor."

Her breath hitched as she looked at him, and for a moment, she saw not just the man who had fought beside her, but the man who had stood by her from the beginning. The one who had believed in her when she had doubted herself. The one who had never given up, even when the odds had seemed impossible. The one who had helped her find the light inside the darkness.

"I don't know if I can ever be free of it," Eleanor whispered, her voice trembling. "I don't know if I can ever truly be rid of what the Hollow has done to me."

Dapo's gaze softened, and he took a step closer to her, his hand reaching up to gently brush her cheek. "You don't have to be rid of it, Eleanor. You just have to learn to live with it. You're not broken. You're whole, even with the darkness inside you. It's part of you, but it doesn't define you."

Her heart twisted in her chest as she looked at him, seeing the depth of his belief in her. His faith was unwavering, like a steady flame in the midst of the storm. The words he spoke—

so simple, so true—seemed to peel away the layers of doubt and fear that had built up inside her over the years. He was right. The Hollow was a part of her, but it wasn't everything. She wasn't defined by her fears, by the darkness that had once consumed her. She was more than that.

Eleanor took a shaky breath, nodding slowly as she tried to steady herself. She wasn't sure how long it would take to heal. How long it would take to learn to live with the shadows in her heart, the scars the Hollow had left behind. But for the first time in what felt like forever, she knew that she could face it. She could face the darkness inside her and still move forward. Because she wasn't alone.

Dapo was with her. Always.

The quiet stretched between them for a moment longer before Eleanor finally spoke, her voice stronger now, though still soft.

"I don't know what comes next, Dapo. I don't know what happens now that the Hollow is gone. But I... I want to try. I want to live, to be free of the fear that has held me captive for so long."

Dapo smiled, a small, tender smile that spoke volumes of the trust and love he had for her. "We'll figure it out together. One step at a time. There's no rush. You've already done the hardest part."

Eleanor looked around the clearing once more, her gaze sweeping over the remnants of their battle. The once-threatening darkness had retreated, but its mark was still visible. The earth was scarred, the trees bent and broken from the force of the Hollow's power. The air was thick with the remnants of magic, the very fabric of reality warped by the events that had transpired.

But even in the wake of destruction, there was a sense of rebirth. A sense that something had shifted, that the world had begun to heal. The sky above them, which had been so dark and heavy just moments ago, was now clearing, the storm clouds parting to reveal a sliver of pale blue. The first light of dawn was breaking through, soft and golden, casting a gentle glow over the wreckage.

"I never thought it would end like this," Eleanor said quietly, her voice full of wonder as she watched the light spread across the sky. "I never thought I'd make it out alive."

"You did," Dapo said simply, squeezing her hand. "You did. And you will keep going."

Eleanor closed her eyes, taking a deep breath as she allowed herself to feel the warmth of the light on her skin. For the first time in a long time, she felt... alive. The weight of the Hollow was still there, lurking in the corners of her soul, but it was no longer the thing that defined her. She had faced it. She had beaten it. And now, she was free to choose what came next.

"I think..." she began, her voice still soft but steady, "I think I'm ready for whatever comes next."

Dapo's eyes softened with something akin to pride, and he nodded, a quiet smile on his lips. "We'll face it together. Whatever it is."

Eleanor took a final, lingering look at the clearing, the place where the Hollow had once been. The place where everything had changed. And as she did, she realized something profound—that while she might carry the scars of her past, the darkness she had fought, she had also gained something irreplaceable. A piece of herself. A piece of strength. And the love of someone who had always believed in her.

The storm had passed. The Hollow was no more. And in its place, there was light.

And that light, Eleanor knew, would always be enough to guide her forward.

Together.

www.ingramcontent.com/pod-product-compliance
Lightning Source LLC
LaVergne TN
LVHW011935070526
838202LV00054B/4655